Discovering

LUTTERWORTH PRESS

HORN

Paula Hardwick

Guildford • Surrey

'It is generally portable, has great variety
and so is very collectable.'

First published 1981

D.O.M.

For my husband
John Audley Hardwick

*The illustration on the half-title page shows a fifteenth-century Scandinavian drinking
horn. The illustration on the title page shows a gemshorn made by Jim Furner from a
European ibex horn.*

ISBN 0–7188–2520–9

Photoset in 12/13pt Bembo by
Nene Phototypesetters Ltd, Northampton

*Printed and bound in Great Britain at
The Camelot Press Ltd, Southampton*

Contents

Foreword

Scotland must take the credit for this book, and Edinburgh in particular, because it was from here that one attractive small horn beaker was taken home at the end of a family holiday. This set me off on a hunt through lending libraries, reference libraries and bookshops for a composite work on horn. There was none. The natural outcome was to carry out research in museums, private collections, libraries, factories, antique shops, Fairs and antiques' centres in various parts of the country, which has resulted in collating material for *Discovering Horn*.

The aim has been to describe some of the uses of horn for social and domestic purposes up to the present day, from animals which include the antelope, buffalo, deer, ox, ram and rhinoceros.

I became amazed at the wide diversity of horn artefacts prepared by the horners when I had researched the material more extensively. There are many people who have contributed information which has helped to put certain facts together; some have a horn collection, others collect a specialized item in different materials including horn, while invaluable background material has been given by people who either work, or have worked certain tools and crafts themselves connected with items in this book.

The glossary of terms may prove useful to the reader who is not familiar with some of the technical words used in the script.

The research is by no means exhaustive, but sets out to encourage the reader to look, question, criticize, conserve and collect!

P.H.   March, 1981

1
HORN in HISTORY

THERE are many cave paintings, carvings and pictorial illustrations of horn and horned animals. Some of the earliest known ones have been found in Spain, France, Italy and Central and Eastern Europe, and are considered to date from about 10,000 BC. It has been shown that there is a fascinating portrayal of animal hierarchy in the presentation of the cave gravings and paintings. The horse, the bison and the wild ox tended to be illustrated in a central position, while the deer, the ibex and the mammoth took a secondary place, although not far removed from the central grouping, whereas the rhinoceros, with the lion and the bear, were only found in the remotest parts of the caves.

Horn was an indispensable natural material of the community from Neolithic times. Archaeologists have found many examples of tools made from antlers dating from this period. Flint mines along the South Downs and at Grimes Caves in Norfolk were worked by Neolithic man with antler tools for digging the flints, while in Yorkshire, for example, an antler mace head was found at Seamer Moor, near Scarborough; a barbed point of antler bone dating from about 8500 BC was found at Starr Carr and an antler harpoon at a cave near Settle. A small adze mounted in antler bone was found at Calfhole cave at Skynethorne and among finds discovered at a barrow dig at Duggleby Howe, North Yorkshire, was a pick and a hammer head shaped from red deer antlers and said to be about 4,000 years old. Examples of similar tools may be found on exhibition in museums throughout the country.

Also found at Starr Carr were some stag antler frontlets. The antlers were still attached to the skull which was perforated to make eyeholes so that the frontlet could be worn as a mask. It is possible that these were used by the hunter as a disguise when he approached his quarry, and they were worn even by children at play. The frontlets were also used at ceremonies in the Greek temples, and at a period as late as the eighteenth century some African engravings feature similar ones.

In early writings by Pliny, Celsus, Caesar and the early Norse runic inscriptions, references are made to the uses of horn both as symbols of power and authority as well as for drinking vessels and medical practices.

Payne's *English Medicine in Anglo-Saxon Times* mentions that horn was used for cupping operations. These cupping horns continued to be made as recently as the nineteenth century and examples may be seen at the Wellcome Historical Medical Museum, London.

Oxhorn was made into many of the essential household articles and one of the earliest surviving is the prehistoric oxhorn spoon dating to 1500 BC held by the Museum of Antiquities, Edinburgh. The spoon measures eleven and a half inches along its entire length and was discovered in its present shape hanging over a clay urn in a cist or prehistoric stone coffin at Broomend, Inverury in 1866, and accounts for the preservation of the horn.

The Tower of London has a number of composite bows which were made from a lamination of horn, wood and sinew, thus providing a very strong combination that was employed particularly in the structure of early crossbows. These were used in China, Persia and Turkey, among other areas.

Some Scandinavian Bronze Age swords have a hilt of horn riveted to the bronze blade and an oak coffin from this period, found in a barrow in Denmark, contained various relics including a horn comb. Rock carvings from the same period also depict horned helmets being worn, and the Vikings are always remembered and illustrated wearing metal horned helmets which were recognized as symbols of strength and superiority.

Because of its cheapness and availability horn became associated with one of the first clearly defined crafts or trades in England. Reference to the craft of the horner is made under the laws of King Ina, *c.* AD 700, to the price at which horn was to be traded: *Bovis cornu decem denariis valeat vaccae cornu duobus denariis valeat.* ('An ox horn is worth 10 denarii, a cow's horn 2 denarii.')

During the Saxon period many of the patens and chalices were made from horn and according to Dr H. G. Rosedale, who was Honorary Chaplain to the Worshipful Company of Horners in 1911,

> At the Council of Chelsea in AD 789, after careful discussion, it was decided that the chalices and patens used for ecclesiastical purposes should no longer be made of horn, but of metal, no doubt to distinguish them from similar articles which had already come into general use for common and domestic purposes.

From the same source one learns that during the Saxon period, the horners, in common practice with other skilled craftsmen, had to be members of a Frith Gild. The Frith Gilds appear to have been agricultural gilds which were forced on the people by their Saxon conquerors. The word gild is derived from the Anglo-Saxon *gildan* or *gildare* meaning to pay and is a reference to the contribution expected from each person towards the common fund.

King Alfred in the ninth century is reputed to be the inventor of the candle-clock; it is said that he surrounded a candle with a funnel of horn to ensure an even rate of burning by excluding draughts. Readers will also discover that during King

(Left) *Fragment from palmate antler, with an engraved figure of a wounded bison. Found at Laugerie Basse cave, Dordogne, France. C. 10,500* BC. *(Right) Prehistoric oxhorn spoon dating to 1500* BC *from Broomend, Inverury, Aberdeenshire. (Maximum length: 29.3 cm.)*

Alfred's reign the City of Ripon was presented with a horn to mark the granting of legal tenure of the Liberty, so freeing it from Royal taxes.

Horns were frequently used as a means of conveyancing land and property in early times rather in the same way as today one would sign and exchange a contract for the conveyancing of land and estate; the Bibliography on page 185 lists written articles which discuss these tenure horns. Among the most well-known is the Pusey horn (now held by the Victoria and Albert Museum) which was owned by the Pusey family in recognition of their ownership of the village of that name. It was given initially by King Canute to a William Pusey as a reward for information received from him when, as a supporter of the Danes, he had dressed as a shepherd and intermingled with the Anglo-Saxons and discovered plans being made to attack King Canute. Edward the Confessor granted the rangership of Bernwode Forest in Buckinghamshire to be held by a horn, while Randal de Meschines, third Earl of Chester, conferred on Allan Silvestris the Bailywick of the Forest of Wirrall by presenting him with a horn.

In Britain the historical connections with horn must include a mention of the drovers, whose routes followed the mediaeval roads (which had developed from the Roman ones), radiating to and from many market towns throughout the country.

The drovers and cattle dealers assembled in districts where large cattle fairs and markets were held. One of these places was Stockbridge, near Winchester, where until the end of the nineteenth century at least thirteen inns existed in the village. One of these which still stands is the Drovers' House in Houghton Road where Welshmen driving sheep to Southampton stayed. Mrs Todd, the present owner of the inn, which is now a private house, understands that the writing on the front of the building is Old Welsh. This has been confirmed by an expert in Old Welsh at the National Museum of Wales in Cardiff who suggests that it is a rhyming couplet, which probably should read:

GWAIR TYMHERUS PORFA FLASUS
temperate hay, tasty pasture
CWRW DA A GWAL CYSURUS
good ale and strawbed comfortable

It is likely that the variation in the spelling found on the building occurred when the inn was refurbished and repainted, prior to which some of the letterings may have become rather faint or even obliterated.

These drovers developed many initiation rituals for newcomers and amongst them was the swearing on the horns before entry as a member of a closely knit 'trade union'. To be sworn in the unfortunate newcomer had to prove his skill in the art of droving by holding a bullock by its horns. This custom appears to have started at a Highgate inn where a group of established cattle drovers resented the intrusion of a stranger to share their room and bar. In later years it became a source of added revenue for the landlord who used it as a means of encouraging travellers to 'stand a jug all round'.

Examples of worked staghorn have survived for many centuries because being bone they are relatively unaffected by variable conditions. Articles from the most commonly used oxhorn made earlier than the seventeenth century are comparatively rare because the composition of the horn was affected by climate and surroundings. Because of this fact it is somewhat difficult to be precise about the peak working period of the horners. However, from documentary evidence, inventories and the number of articles surviving, it would seem reasonable to suggest that the highlight period of the horn industry came between the beginning of the seventeenth century and the first half of the nineteenth century. Examples are found outside these periods in both directions, but not in sufficient quantity to justify the extension in time.

2
The CRAFT of the HORNER

To become a master horner in the seventeenth century on an independent basis needed a financial backing of more than a hundred pounds. At this time it was estimated that about seven hundred thousand horns were required annually to cope with the needs of the twenty-four master horners. Among the earliest better known names of horn workers rank Robart Mindum for his highly graved shoe horns, John Obrisset for his boxes and John Osborn, an Englishman from Worcestershire working in Amsterdam in 1626, for his medallions. There is a signed piece made by him in the Franks Collection at the British Museum with a portrait of Princess Amelia of Orange. The inscription on the reverse side reads: FRED HENRICVS D.G. PRINCEPS AVRIACAE COMES NASSOVIA ETC IOH OSBORN ANGL AMSTEROD FECIT 1626.

As described in the chapter on the brief History of the Horners' Company there was great demand for the English horn to be sold abroad and in spite of laws trying to curtail this activity the trade clearly went on in some quantity. London was the world centre in the early days for the distribution of raw horn from a number of countries including Africa and continental buyers came over for their supplies on a regular basis. Monsieur Roubo, in the eighteenth century, mentions 'Corne d'Angleterre'. He favoured the use of the very fine translucent horn which was used to imitate lacquer work. Poller describes the procedure which is very similar to the Boulle technique where these thin leaves could be coloured with pigment on the underside, a special paper added to distribute evenly the green or blue pigment and to ensure that a perfect contact was made when finally the combined layers were glued to the basic framework, generally of oak.

In the eighteenth century Collyer, in his book on *The Parents and Guardians Directory of a Profession or Trade*, said of the horner's craft:

> This is an ingenius though a stinking business which requires more ingenuity than strength.

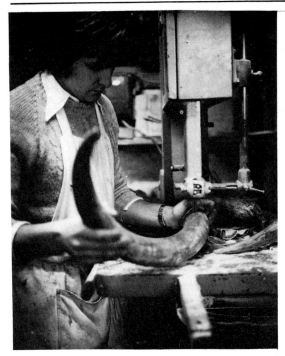

(Left) *Sawing horn requires a skill which is based on a judgement of each horn's shape and weight.* (Right) *Heating horn by means of a gas flame, which softens the material before it is flattened or moulded into plates.*

He described the horn presser as

> a person requiring more strength than ingenuity.

In Campbell's book published in 1747 called *The London Tradesman*, which was written to help young people to choose a suitable trade or profession, he stated:

> The horner is likewise kindred to the turner as he turns a great many of the articles he deals in, which are both numerous and useful. It is none of the most polite trades, though a very useful one, for the stench of horn which they sometimes manufacture with the heat of the fire keeps them from the Hyp, Vapours and Lowness of Spirits, the Common Malady of England. A lad, if of a middling strong make, may be found at fourteen years of age, and when out of his time earns from twelve to eighteen shillings a week.

It is worth quoting Campbell's comments of the turner as the work entailed often directly relates to horn.

> The Turner's trade is a very ingenius Business, and brought to great perfection in this Kingdom. He makes use of an Engine called a Lathe; his work is fixed in it upon a Center, and is turned by a String, which either goes round the Work, if it turns upon

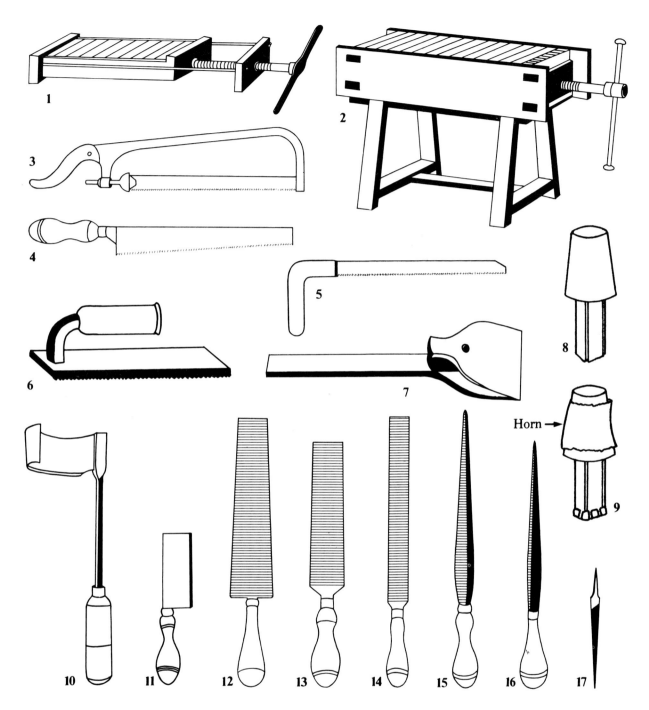

1. Table top box press for flattening heated plates of horn until cooled; 2. Bench structure box press; 3,4. Hand saws; 5. Angled cutting knife with fine saw edge for cutting section of horn; 6. Small rasp for removing rough outer surface; 7. Wooden clamp for flattening of single plate until cooled; 8,9. Metal formers for shaping heated section of beaker; 10. Prising tool for flattening angle of heated horn; 11. Small scraper for levelling surface of plate; 12,13,14. Three files for smoothing processes known as grailing; 15. Coarse file for shaping teeth of comb; 16,17. Fine files for shaping teeth of comb.

Horn →

two Pivots, or round a Wheel, fixed to the moving Center. There are several sorts of Lathes, which differ according to the Nature of the Work they are to perform; but they all agree in common Principles.

Turners differ among themselves according to the Materials they Use; some turn Wood, others Ivory, Tortoise-shell, etc. and others Metal, Iron, Brass, Gold or Silver. All branches of the Work are profitable but those who work in Toys made of rich materials earn more than those who work in wood, and form more necessary Utensils.

. . . The Engines used in the nicer sort of Turning are very expensive, therefore it requires a good Stock to set up with, and a natural Genius for this Art to become Eminent in it. There is an infinite Variety in their Work, and they must be learning all their Life. A Boy may be found about Fourteen or Fifteen, ought to be pretty robust in his Constitution, and his Education that of a Common Tradesman.

In the early days horns were often soaked for a period of months to encourage the separation from the core. The horns were afterwards sorted according to size and quality. The next stage was for the presser to cut off the solid horn tips before dividing the horns by sawing into varying lengths. Each section would then be cut along its natural curve and afterwards soaked in hot water or oil for a time which considerably softened it before it was subjected to a fire where the constant movement over the flame prevented any scorching taking place, but made the horn very malleable, after which it could be more easily pulled open by the use of pincers. It was then spread nearly flat and placed between hot iron plates, previously coated with tallow and pressed with great force. The amount of pressure varied dependant upon the thinness required. Further scraping could be done by hand using a draw-knife having a wire edge, particularly if the plates were to be used for any very fine work or where translucency was an all-important factor as in lanthorn leaves. In other words, the presser made the leaves which were then converted into useful articles by other craftsmen either at home or abroad.

The horner may have bought these leaves if they were not made on his own premises and moulded and turned them to make boxes, handles, spoons and other useful articles. The product required polishing which was done by using perhaps either very finely ground charcoal with water, or with pumice powder, before using wood ash as a finisher, followed by a chamois leather and finally the hand.

Horners are known to have worked from very early times, but the main manufacturing centres in England from the thirteenth century (with some interruptions) appear to have been in London, Sheffield and York and, from the eighteenth century in Aberdeen, Bewdley, Birmingham, Bradford, Gloucester and Kendal.

Today there are still horn factories on the continent in France, Germany and Italy and there is a flourishing horn export trade from Hong Kong, India and Korea besides the British commercial manufacturers in Dykehead, Scotland, and other areas including Birmingham and Kendal. The American markets appear to rely on imports from these sources, particularly from the British factories.

3
TYPES of HORN

THE types of horn being described are limited to those which grow on the upper part of the skull of the bovidae group of animals and to certain hoofed animals most commonly handled by the horners for their artefacts.

Stag horn, although true bone, was a frequent medium for the horners' expertise and was not an expensive commodity like tortoiseshell. The latter is being excluded from discussion, apart from various general comments necessary for comparison, as it deserves to be researched separately.

Horn is made up of stratified layers of keratose material and is attached to the skull with the inner bone core. Horn, being a thermoplastic substance, may be moulded, cut, shaped and polished successfully; but care must be taken with the

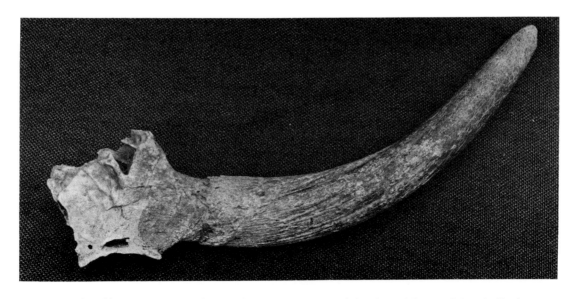

An example of horn core. It is formed by an extension of the frontal bone of the skull, the covering of which is the sheath or true horn. (Overall length 33 cm, horn core only 22.9 cm.)

process of heating, as underheating will allow it to return to its original form and overheating will make it lose its strength and so become brittle.

The reduction in the size of horn growth has been intentionally brought about by the breeders today so that the animal cannot harm its fellow creatures and so spoil the flesh which would lower the market value. It is also known that horn growth does take strength from the animals. It naturally follows that if animals are slaughtered at an earlier age horn growth will be reduced as well, even without the artificial help from hormones.

Horn reacts very like human hair in its quality. If the feeding is good and the health is good, the horn will be good. Some of the best horn, which is invariably white oxhorn, comes from South Africa, especially the Transvaal. Conversely, the Nigerian horn, where the feeding conditions are less favourable, tends to be poor in quality and rather brittle. It is therefore very important for the buyer of horn in any quantity to know and have absolute faith in the dealer from abroad who must be prepared to maintain a high standard quality control.

ANTELOPE

Antelope covers the various species which include the tiny dik-dik, the duiker, and the gazelle. Dik-diks are found in South-West Africa, in East Africa, Somalia and eastern Ethiopia. Duikers come from the African forests. The word comes from the Afrikaans word meaning 'diver', which is a reference to the way the animal will make a dash for cover when disturbed. All these species have a dark, straight horn which is ringed and notched to within a short distance (approximately 1½ in.) from the tip, where it is smooth. These horns are bought from any available source for use by craftsmen.

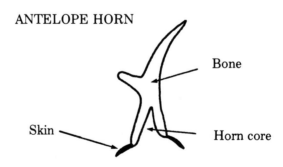

ANTELOPE HORN

Bone

Skin

Horn core

The Rocky mountain goat is being included in this group as it belongs to the chamois family and is not a true goat. The horns of this animal are dark with a slight curve in the tip. These horns have been used frequently by the Canadian Indians for making a great variety of spoons and scoops. Some beautifully carved examples may be seen in the Royal Ontario Museum.

Dik-dik horns have a narrow core which, when removed, leaves an ideal, small, hollow vessel for the craftsman to develop into a useful domestic article like the container for needles illustrated with the bone scrimshaw cap.

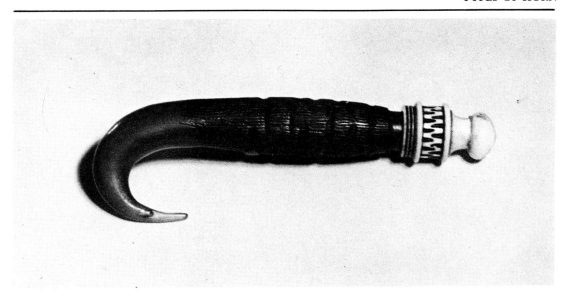

Nineteenth-century dik-dik horn needle case with bone scrimshaw cap.

BUFFALO

Buffalo horns for manufacturing purposes come mostly from India and Thailand. These horns are from the Asian buffalo bred for domestic purposes and they are widely used because the animal is not a protected species like its African counterpart. In their basic state the horns have a quantity of ridging which makes them more difficult to work – the horns are large, somewhat flattened and dark. Some buffalo horn is supplied from Egypt and this can be distinguished by an expert because of the grey rings within the mottling, while the most prized type comes from Thailand, sometimes of a watery green hue. Once the horns have been worked these shadings become particularly attractive.

BUFFALO HORN

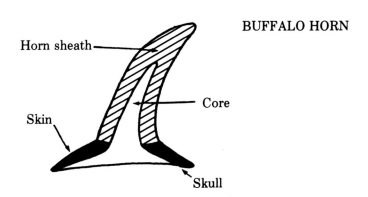

19

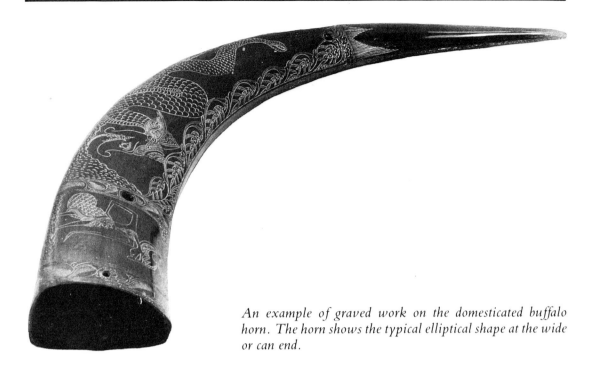

An example of graved work on the domesticated buffalo horn. The horn shows the typical elliptical shape at the wide or can end.

Some public buildings today have handles on the glass doors made from complete buffalo horns. The shape is good, and the horn responds well to the automatic polishing from the frequent touch of the human hand.

Sectional cuts of buffalo horn are used for many purposes including buttons, combs, gun butts, plain umbrella handles, boxes and scales. Because of its hardness it is useful as a stopper for many purposes, one obvious one being for the powder horn. This horn has never been used for lanthorn leaves because of the considerable difficulty encountered when trying to split it and also because of the depth of colour.

Confusion sometimes arises between oxhorn and buffalo horn. With whole horns it is practically impossible to make a mistake once the two different types have been seen together. The buffalo is eliptical in shape, thicker in its wall structure and quite heavily ridged along the inner side of the curve as it widens towards the can end, whereas the oxhorn is more cylindrical in form at this end and without the heavy ridging.

Small buffalo horn boxes with brass studding are now being manufactured in India from the horn tips of these animals. The boxes are retailing in the High Street shops for a little under two pounds, but regrettably are finding their way into the antique markets. If the inside of the box is examined it will appear grey in colour and show no signs of wear or age.

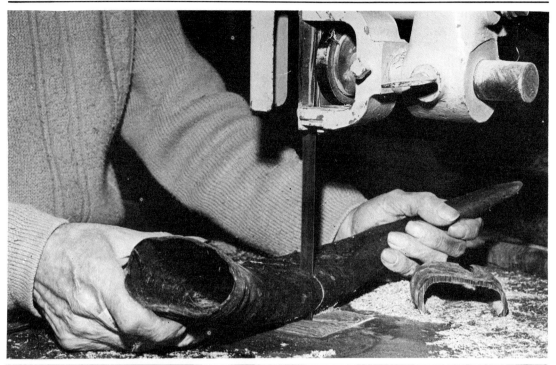

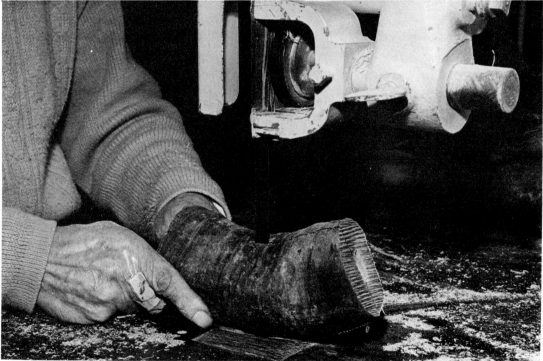

(Above) *The solid tip of horn is cut, leaving the hollow section.*
(Below) *The hollow section is then cut into two halves and flattened for various uses.*

OXHORN

The type of horn produced by cows and bulls varies from one country to another depending on the breeding ground and climatic conditions. South Africa produces very good horns varying in length from 30–50 in. each, but regrettably the output has been reduced because of the modernized breeding methods and the increased use of the tractor. The latter dispenses with the necessity for the older animals, who in time past, pulled the plough. The West African countries produce a rather stringy and brittle horn which, although of good length, is not particularly suited to development by the craftsman. One of the best types of horn came from Angola, but at the present time supplies are not available from this source.

The South Americans, who were previously suppliers to the raw horn companies, have adopted the fairly widespread practice of cutting off the horn tips which prevents injury to the hides. This, of course, ruins the sheath as a saleable commodity other than for fertilizer use, because the horn will split at the edges.

Oxhorns are usually distinguishable because of their pale colouring which is often streaked with stronger, warmer colourings ranging from pale creamy white, to a reddish brown, through to black. The amount of colouring varies considerably. The very good horn from Australian oxen has the milk-white colouring which is always in demand for the high grade comb.

The longhorn cattle produce horns of very fine texture which are free from any black colour. When polished they sometimes present an almost translucent green.

The sheath may be separated from the pith or core by heating the total horn in water and pulling off the sheath. Alternatively, the two parts will readily separate after a few days of natural drying in good warm even conditions.

The solid tip of the horn which is used for button-manufacture and handle-hafting varies in length from 4–10 in., with an average of 4–5 in.

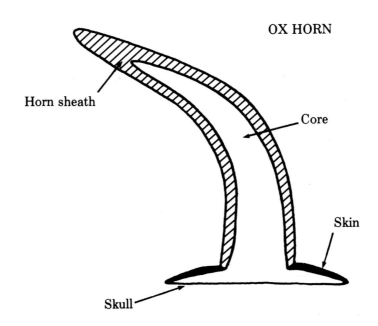

OX HORN

Horn sheath

Core

Skin

Skull

RAM

The main supplies of rams' horns for the British market come from North Africa, although a limited number are supplied to the smaller English horners from our own flocks. These include the Herdwick, one of the many mixed breeds resulting from a cross between the black-faced sheep of the Pennines and the Scandinavian tan-faced sheep which the Vikings brought to this country. The Herdwicks are found not only in the Lake District but also in the south-west of England. Other breeds include the Swaledale, the Jacob, the Cheviot and the Portland.

A species of wild sheep called the mouflon is found on the mountain slopes of both Corsica and Sardinia and another similar species is found in Turkey and Cyprus. The horns from the mouflon may easily be mistaken for the more common ram's horn apart from the variation in size – those of the mouflon being much larger. The Soay, which is similar in appearance to the mouflon, but smaller, is found mostly in the Outer Hebrides and the heavy horns from the Soay do not have a spiral twist which is common to both the general breeds of the ram and mouflon. The shadings in all instances tend to be of a uniform greenish or brownish hue.

It is quite difficult to find good quality rams' horns for they are not infrequently damaged during the lifetime of the animal. In many instances the farmers may have treated them, for example by removing the tip to prevent damage to other members of the flock. The angulated horns which are marked by transverse wrinkles may also be subjected to specialist treatment for show purposes, one of the favourite techniques being the application of a hot swede which can heat the horn so that the shape may be adjusted.

Rams' horns are used by the stick-dressers, by horners for making the modern shofarot and by the golf club craftsmen who use a wedge of horn beautifully inserted into the prepared side of the putter which addresses the ball.

It is a very resistant type of horn and is among the most difficult to work. Nevertheless it will respond well to the expert horner and the results of endless hours of preparation provide a very beautiful object for the owner and the onlooker.

RHINOCEROS

The rhinoceros has been overhunted for many years, although it is now a protected species. On account of this rhinoceros horns are very rare and prized.

The horn is made up of solidified, hair-like fibres which grow from the skin. It is not a structure growing from the skull as in the bovidae group of animals and the horn has no core.

Rhinoceroses were once fairly widespread in India but now the majority of them are found in Assam, and only there in very limited numbers. It must be remembered that the Indian rhinoceros is a single-horned animal whereas the Sumatran species has two horns like its African counterpart.

The African black rhinoceros is now confined mainly to the north-west corner of the continent. The white rhinoceros, which has the larger horns, was in danger of total extinction until more rigid security was mounted. Some herds have now increased their numbers to the extent that a few can be moved to stock new game reserves.

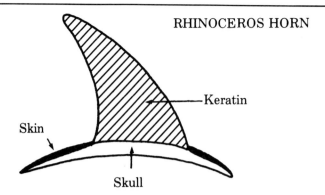

RHINOCEROS HORN

Keratin

Skin

Skull

The latest demand for this horn comes from Arab countries where it is much sought after for the hilts of ceremonial daggers.

In April 1979 one hundred and forty-one horns from Kenya were confiscated in West Germany. On the black market twenty-six pounds weight of horn was worth a quarter of a million pounds sterling, which made it twice as valuable as gold, ounce for ounce, at that time.

The horn may be ground into powder for love philtres and put into libation cups often made of rhinoceros horn. This is a practice still used in Japan as well as the Middle East.

(Left) *Rhinoceros horn, showing the solid mass of hair-like structures which grow as a direct extension of the epidermis. (Vertical height: 29.5 cm, maximum base width: 13.0 cm.)*
(Right) *Magnification of section of rhinoceros horn to show hair-like structure.*

(Left) Buffalo hoof horn in its natural state. (Right) Calf's hoof horn snuff box, the lid of which is metal hinged. (Length: 5.7 cm.)

HOOF

Hooves of the bovidae group of animals are obtained from many parts of the world, but perhaps especially from Russia, India, Pakistan, and South America. The hooves are now only used for making the ground powder which is sold for its nitrogenous content to the fertilizer manufacturers.

There are still quite a number of examples of hoof-horn snuff boxes about. Being a more malleable type of horn because of its thinner surface and because of its natural shape, the horner did not require the same skill to make something of it. The photograph shows a calf's hoof-horn, the lid of which is metal hinged. In the open position the lid lining shows the horn striations particularly well. This has occurred probably because the edges were not smoothed off correctly in the first place so that a split developed from a rough edge, rather in the same manner as a finger nail may split if not cut or filed correctly.

Some of these hoof-horns are tipped with metal, and of course, the size of hoof in many examples shows a natural variety in size and colour. None of them is stained, but one example seen at Chelsea Antiques Fair in 1979 had been painstakingly nailed with fine copper nails all along the outer edge of the lid and the hinge was also made from copper; the base edge was tipped with the same metal.

DEER

Deer horns grow in an amazing variety of ways on innumerable types of species found over a wide area of the world. Most antlers for commercial purposes in this country come from the Muntjac and Sambar deer of India, from the Scottish deer, those of New Zealand and also from the continent, especially Switzerland. Probably the finest antlers come from the West European red deer in France, Germany and Denmark. When a stag has a total of twelve tines he is known as a royal. If he presents fourteen he is known as an imperial. The number of tines varies from one beast to another, but there are usually five or more on each side.

25

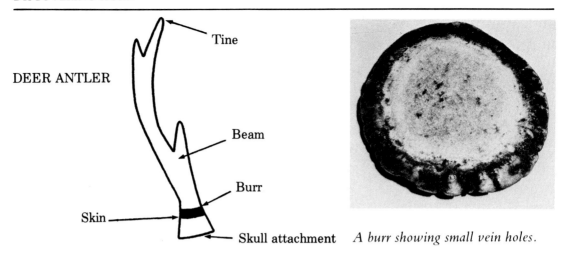

DEER ANTLER

Tine

Beam

Burr

Skin

Skull attachment

A burr showing small vein holes.

The fallow deer which is a native of southern Europe may easily be distinguished by the palmate antlers, so called because of the similarity to the palm of the hand, with a number of points extending to give the impression of fingers. The antlers from fallow deer are shed annually in May.

Reindeer horn is little used because of its uneven form and it is generally considered to be unattractive.

Staghorn and deer horns consist entirely of bone, with only a pencil line pith. The circular ridge called the burr appears a short distance from the base of the antler and divides the antler into pedicel on the skull side of the burr and beam on the far side. Small vein holes may be seen on a burr as the illustration shows. As maturation takes place the circulation in the beam diminishes and the velvet skin dries and peels off, leaving the fully developed but dead antler bone. The antlers are shed, usually between the months of February and May. As the year ends, sloughing takes place on the pedicel side so that the beam and burr are shed and the end of the pedicel heals over. The new growth process restarts.

The antlers removed from a shot deer are easily distinguishable because part of the skull is attached beyond the burr which of course does not take place when the shedding takes place naturally.

Richard Perry, the naturalist, has written a charming story of the four seasons in the everyday life of the red deer herds in Scotland. He points out that before the devastation of the forests in the nineteenth century, when feeding conditions were easier, it was not uncommon to find a big forest stag with twenty tines or more on its antlers. A pair of mounted antlers with that number would indeed be a treasure for the collector. Nature has adjusted to the present living conditions by reducing the overall weight of the animal, and since so much strength goes into antler development this has necessarily been adjusted too. The following picture shows very clearly why diet plays an important part in bone development and where deer are concerned this affects their usefulness for commercial purposes. The Scots tine is too porous, and compression to make it solid is impossible. When hafting for

26

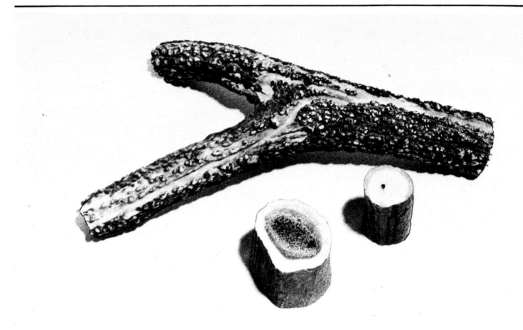

Section of antler beam showing depressions where the venous supply was carried during growth, with two sections of tines, one of porous growth resulting from poor feeding, the other a closely knit example resulting from good feeding.

commercial purposes an epoxy resin may be used, but is not very satisfactory as water will eventually seep into the gaps of the open flint-type pith. The Nepalese example shows good bone growth which is ideal for hafting as the drill will not splinter this type, and the finished result is far more pleasing and satisfactory, and the glue is not disturbed.

The antlers, as they loosen, often become irritating and it is then that the stag will thrash around in heather and tussocks to try to be rid of them. The animals also make use of their special peat hags for this purpose, as well as to relieve the irritation of the warble fly.

Mention must be made here of the giant deer, otherwise known as the Irish elk, which lived eleven to twelve thousand years ago. Remains of these deer have been found in over two hundred places in Ireland, especially in Balleybetagh bog near Dublin and in County Limerick. It is a possibility that the antlers may also have been shed in these bogs for the same reasons referred to above.

At the end of the nineteenth century the heavily antlered skulls of these deer were so much in demand for country house adornment that a number of one-man industries for this trade were set up near Dublin. The antler span was sometimes as much as eleven feet and the term Irish elk has been used for the finds occasionally. The antlers were located in the bogs by the use of long metal probes.

Stag horn is nearly always richly granulated on its surface and has a greater density of colour when compared with that of the common deer which is much smoother. Through usage stage horn acquires a rich sheen on its prominent parts and this richness in colour may be seen in deer horn too. The old custom was to subject these antlers to the tan pit in order to improve the colour before being divided into sections for various articles.

'The Vikings' Exhibition held in the British Museum during 1980 showed very finely worked antler moulds which were used for mass-producing cheap brooches of tin and pewter, some examples of which were on display.

Antler horn was used and worked with great skill by specialized craftsmen in Viking towns and among articles found, like pins, toggles, dress fasteners, handles, dice, playing pieces and weaving tools, was the comb. This appears to be the most commonly found item for household use and among the exhibits one discovered that the more complex combs were made from a series of plates fastened on either side by ribs which were held together by rivets; the teeth were delicately sawn after assembly and the finished product was sometimes protected by a comb-case.

The use of hartshorn (more commonly known today as smelling salts) is described from Anglo-Saxon times and is still used in some countries today, including Japan, as an aphrodisiac.

In New Zealand deer farming for the velvet is now quite big business, according to their Department of Trade and Industry. The velvet is dried and exported to South-east Asia. Crushed deer and ram's horn goes to the same area also for use as an aphrodisiac.

It would appear that the total trade in horn going to Japan, Korea and Hong Kong, with a smaller amount to Germany and Australia, totals some two hundred million New Zealand dollars per annum.

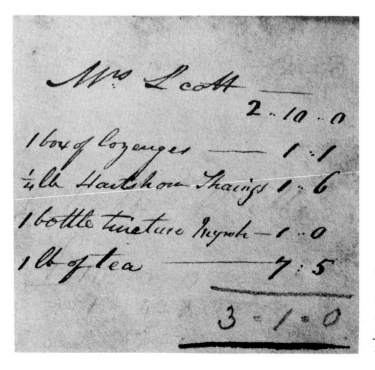

An account taken from a Calendar of 1821 compiled by John Watson Stewart of Dublin, showing quantities of hartshorn shavings and tincture of myrrh for use in the preparation of smelling salts.

4
DRINKING HORNS

Drinking horns are recorded by Sir Charles Oman as being 'in use in classical times and many primitive peoples have used drinking horns since then'. From Caesar one finds that the Germans drank from horns tipped with silver, while in the National Museum, Copenhagen, there are quite a few examples from the Roman period, although in most cases only the bronze mountings have survived.

In the British Museum there are fragments of four Anglo-Saxon drinking horns, with the original gilt-bronze mounts dating from the first half of the seventh century, which were found in a sealed bronze container inside a grave at Taplow Court, Buckinghamshire in 1883. The Museum also has reconstructed two Anglo-Saxon drinking horns, but using the original mounts, from the Sutton Hoo Ship Burial near Woodbridge in Suffolk. The photograph shows a seventh-century AD die made from bronze. 'Strips of gold foil would be hammered

Bronze die AD 700. Used for stamping out decorations in metal for addition to drinking horns.

on to this which would receive the imprint of the interlaced biting animals. The foil probably decorated the drinking horns and wooden bottles similar to those found at Sutton Hoo.' This example, with the caption quoted, may be seen at the Moyse's Hall Museum, Bury St Edmunds.

The Bayeux tapestry is often cited for its picture of Harold and his men using drinking horns at a banquet at Bosham, near Chichester. These do not appear to have any supports to keep the wide end aloft and it must be supposed the contents had either to be drunk in a single draught, or the horn held in the hand.

Probably the earliest date of a known, surviving drinking horn with feet is the one in the possession of Corpus Christi College, Cambridge. The horn dates from the fourteenth century and was acquired by the College at its foundation in 1352. Queen's College, Oxford has one dating from approximately the same period, while Christ's Hospital, Horsham, has a horn with silver gilt mounts dating from the end of the fifteenth century. There are a number of other known vessels which, like the ones mentioned, have been ably described by other writers on the subject of medieval drinking horns. For those who wish to read about these in more detail, please refer to the Bibliography. Not all early decorated drinking horns were actually used for that purpose. Many were given or received as a symbol of the right to hold office or an estate, and are known as tenure horns.

Very often the mountings on these horns are simple, while others show a Gothic influence, as for example the one in the possession of the Victoria and Albert Museum dating from the fifteenth century. It is a most attractive curved oxhorn mounted with bands of gilt bronze, joined by strips of metal, which would have originally numbered four at each quarter of the round, as remaining hinges indicate very clearly at the wide end. Some of these hinges are copper based while others are brass. The wide end is inscribed in Gothic lettering GOT HELP MIR ('Dear God help me') and the words are interspersed with leaf patterning. The waist band has two hollow stands welded to it but these are not a matching pair. Facing the outside curve, the right one has four ring turnings. The tip end stand, forming an open petalled flower of metal, is welded to two short strips joining the longer ones running along the sides to a plainer metal band at the narrowing tip, the very end of which is mounted by a boss and flower. (*See* illustration on page 1.)

All the gilt-bronze metalwork has scallop work along its main edges with a recurring leaf pattern which is repeated in reduced form at the boss below the flower stem.

(Opposite) *Seventeenth-century Dutch drinking horn with whistle tip silver mount.*

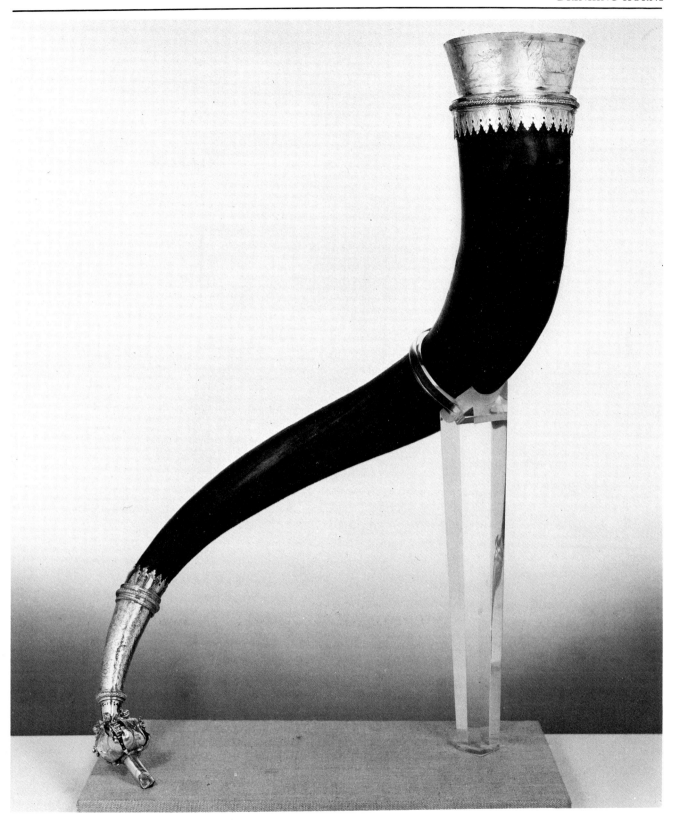

Drinking horns of this design are typical of Scandinavia and there are very similar ones in both the University of Oslo and the British Museum, although the latter is smaller in proportion and has claw feet.

The Victoria and Albert Museum possesses another magnificent example of an early seventeenth century oxhorn drinking horn with the silver mount at the wide end depicting the chase and incorporating a graving of a church, a rabbit, a stag in flight, two men and a dog and a sitting bear watching the progress of a huntsman with two hounds partially hidden by a tree. The tip end is silver, mounted with a whistle and, according to the caption:

> The graving incorporates floral scrolls, the whistle protruding from four leaves graved with chevrons, which alternate with brackets surmounted by human heads. The maker's mark, a gate: Date, letter M. Dutch (Franeker mark); about 1615.

The next section shows how this combined technique of drinking horn and whistle was used in Scotland in the seventeenth and eighteenth centuries.

Conical drinking horns

A conical drinking horn would be fashioned from oxhorn which had been cut to a suitable length from a fairly young horn with very little solid tip. This section would then be heated and moulded to shape on a former, very often made of wood, where it would be left until the horn was absolutely cold. The horn would then be cleaned and partially polished, after which the horner, having decided on the form of decoration, could then proceed with either graving, or turning, and for this purpose the wide end of the horn would be fixed to the mandrel of a lathe. Following this came the final buffing and polishing to make the horn ready for use. Some of the decorative work was beautifully executed and there are a number of very fine seventeenth and eighteenth century examples. The patination and toning of the natural oxhorn to a burnished cream through to brown would be difficult to imitate and the gravings and turnings have lost all traces of sharpness, leaving only the well recognized signs of wear which are familiar, in the same way, to an expert who is used to handling early workings and carvings in wood.

These conical horns are sometimes found with a whistle carved at the tip. They could thus serve two very practical purposes, which provided the highland farmer, or in fact any

hill traveller, with an ideal article for everyday use. They seem to be a peculiarly Scottish innovation which was surprisingly not copied south of the Border.

One of these drinking horns has been seen with the later addition of a cork bung and leather thonging, attached to which is a wooden spoon, the clear indication being that it is a snuff mull! The beautiful turnings on the horn work when compared with the crude workmanship of the spoon immediately raised suspicions and the original use of the horn is now probably held in very little doubt by anyone. On another occasion a conical horn was examined with fine graving work dated 1623. At a later date, probably in the early nineteenth century, this vessel was capped to form a mull with a crude brass, hinged lid.

(Left) *Engraved seventeenth-century conical drinking horn with turned solid tip. Inscribed I.A. 1699 REMME, B.N. (Approx. length: 22 cm.)*
(Centre) *Early eighteenth-century conical drinking horn with scallop scroll graving and whistle tip. (Length: 22.3 cm.)*
(Right) *Early eighteenth-century, turned, conical drinking horn with silver rim and the initials DG. The tip end has a finely worked whistle. The inside of the oxhorn is dark, but has faded to a green toning on the outer surfaces. (Approx. length: 10.6 cm.)*

33

Because metal pins have been used to hold the brasswork to the horn, restoration to its rightful origin will never be fully satisfactory.

Rhinoceros horn cups

Rhinoceros horn cups were made in large numbers from the Tang dynasty (AD 618–906) up to the present day, and it is from China that the great majority of carved examples come, although cups have been worked occasionally by Europeans. Mr Soames Jenyns, an acknowledged expert in the field of oriental antiquities, points this out in his comprehensive chapter 'Carvings in Ivory and Rhinoceros Horn' in *Chinese Art*.

The cups are often referred to as libation cups because they were used to carry a drink-offering to honour the gods, or as a ceremonial act in honour of the dead, and at other times they were carried at banquets and feasts.

It would appear that the strange and mythical connections attached to the rhinoceros horn all date back to the Chinese. The trade in libation cups spread the stories and it is well known that they were used for detecting poisons. It was

Libation cup of lobed foliate form, the exterior carved with brambles, berries and flowerheads. Chinese c. 1700. (Length: 15.5 cm.)

believed that if a liquid was placed in the cup, any subsequent frothing would indicate that it was poisonous. Scientists have suggested that with a strongly alkaline drink the horn could react, thus producing the froth. It was also believed that if a poisoned wound was touched by a cup relief would be obtained. Other medical purposes for which this horn was used included the treatment of epilepsy, labour pains and paralysis.

The earliest surviving cups are undecorated, but carved decoration is to be found in some form on the majority of the later examples. By the early nineteenth century the carvings became very elaborate when Cantonese craftsmen began producing them for export.

The horns were nearly always carved to include dragons representing mythology and the lotus to represent Buddhism.

When the horn is first cut and polished it has a yellowish toning and great variety in the grey streaking and mottling. But the beautiful amber hue, which is the usual colour, is achieved by staining and further burnishing. This, together with the carvings and various decorations, make it a vessel of unusual charm.

Eighteenth-century fine quality rhinoceros horn cup with intricate carving both inside and outside to represent a lotus flower.

These enchanting little vessels which deserve a special mention are documented and displayed at the Museum of Antiquities in Edinburgh.

The quaich comes from the Gaelic word *cuach* which means a cup and was made originally from wood with a lug or handle extended on either side of the central bowl. As the years went by the quaich was made from pewter, brass, silver and horn as well as other materials. It continued in popular use until the nineteenth century. From this time on the quaich became a frequent choice for prizes and presentation pieces and examples are to be found on the market in both translucent and natural oxhorn with turned outer sides, the inner central bowl base being mounted with a metal disc with the inscription in Gaelic SGUAB AS'I which means 'drink heartily' or 'drink it up'. Sometimes each of the lugs may have a further silver mount, perhaps with interlace work or the Celtic cross, while others have a silver metal mount holding a gemstone in position.

The Museum of Antiquities has an exquisite eighteenth-century example of a deep quaich in translucent oxhorn with symmetrical pin-graving on the outside of the bowl. The lugs are line-pressed with pin marks where they meet the bowl. There is slight damage to the lip edge on one side.

Quaichs

Translucent oxhorn quaich (c. 1900) with turned base and silver mount inscribed SGUAB AS' I and marked WD & Co. The lugs have silver mounts inset with cairngorms. (Maximum length: 13 cm.)

In the churchyard at Tranent, East Lothian, a tombstone states 'David Mather, Quaichmaker, who died in 1687'. The tombstone also shows examples of the tools required for the trade. Records kept at Edinburgh show that quaichmakers were active there in 1696 and in Aberdeen in 1719.

The novelist Tobias Smollet in the eighteenth century wrote in *Humphrey Clinker*:

> When the Lowlanders want a cheerupping cup, they go to the public house called the Change-house, and call for a chopin (a measure) of twopenny, which is a thin yeasty beverage, made of malt; not quite so strong as the table beer of England. This is brought in a pewter stoop, shaped like a skittle, from whence it is emptied into a quaff; that is a curious cup made of different pieces of wood, such as box and ebony, cut into little staves, joined alternately and secured with delicate hoops, having two ears or handles. It holds about a gill, is sometimes tipped around the mouth with silver and has a plate of the same metal at the bottom, with the landlord's cipher engraved.

Fine eighteenth-century oxhorn quaich with pin graving. (Length: 11 cm.)

Quaichs are ideal containers for various purposes in the home, from flower arranging to storing bon-bons. Some collectors, however, may feel that they have a beauty of their own which should remain unadorned! Beware of the cigarette smoker who may consider it makes an ideal ash-tray, for the resulting scorch mark is difficult to treat.

Beakers

Beakers were the conventional drinking vessels for everyday use from the seventeenth century, coming as a natural development from drinking horns which were more difficult to handle. A horn beaker was made by forcing a section of unslit heated horn on to a wooden or metal former. When cooled, the beaker cylinder was removed from the conical form and turned on a lathe to smooth all its rough surfaces. A groove was then made on the inside of the narrow end to take the horn disc, which could also be turned on a lathe. Sometimes a glass base was used instead. Insertion was achieved by holding the end of the beaker over a fire until sufficiently malleable to permit the slipping of the base into position in the groove. On cooling and consequent contraction of the horn the base became firmly fixed. (Spectacles and magnifying glasses are fixed by a similar method.) Horners liked to have a distinguishing feature on their own beaker bases and various turnings illustrate this. Others used their name or initials.

A selection of wooden formers used for moulding and turning various artefacts including beakers.

A pair of fine quality silver-lined oxhorn beakers with the mark I.P and oval escutcheons each graved with a leopard. C. 1800. (Maximum height: 12.9 cm, diameter: 9 cm.)

(Below) *Mid nineteenth-century ox-horn goblet with turned stem and base. (Height: 18.8 cm.)*

The final polish varies according to the horn and the horner. It was often done by using pulverized rottenstone and oil, or by using soft soap with the natural grease of the hand.

Many of these beakers are made from a variety of oxhorn and the colourings are wide-ranging and very attractive. Very few of them are stained, but examples have been examined where the desire is clearly to simulate tortoiseshell. It is particularly unfortunate that this has been done with some of the small beakers as they were originally translucent horn medicine beakers. (For details of this technique, refer to Chapter 7, 'Staining and Dyeing'.)

Some beakers are mounted with silver rims, and some are even silver lined. Occasionally shields were added with family crests engraved upon them. The silver may or may not be hallmarked as it took anything up to six months for the Assay Office to check the silver and give it the necessary guarantee. There is a splendid example of a tall, silver-rimmed beaker in the Victoria and Albert Museum. Engraved on the silver is the following:

This was of an ox that weighed 351st. 2lbs. whereof the tallow was 21st. 7lbs. blood and kidneys not weighed. Killed by Sr Richd Osbaldeston Jan 28 170$^6_9$.

It may be seen in the Metalwork Department.

Hunting scenes were very popular gravings on beakers and York Castle and Hereford Museums have a number of rather fine examples. Besides hunting scenes, the graver busied himself with geometrical and floral designs on these beakers; others depict wild animals and many reflect the probable occupations of their original owners like the harvester, with his sickle, fork, rake and flail. The mail coach, fishing, the races, gardening, hunting, Regency country house scenes and windmills are frequent, while the typical British scene of the village cricketer has also been depicted. The standard of graving varies considerably and the continuity of the scene does too.

Many have decorative scroll work at the top and the base which is more or less identical in form. One of these has been seen with a mounting of silver covering the scrollwork with a silver hallmark of 1820. This helps to date some of these beakers fairly conclusively into the period of the early nineteenth century. Engraved date marking must always be viewed with a certain scepticism as the desire to make something appear to be earlier is not a practice peculiar to this age! Regrettably there is a ready market for 'faked' early graving, the work being undertaken on beakers of some age, but the standard of graving and the 'wear' is at variance with the suggested dating. Supplies are coming from both the Birmingham and London areas.

Occasionally beakers were made to take apart for ease of carrying and this required very precise workmanship in order

Beautifully graved white oxhorn beaker inscribed 'To commemorate Thee landing of George the Fourth in Scotland.' and 'A vew of Leith Roads'. Red ink used for loopwork below pewter rim and also for boat. (Maximum height: 12 cm, diameter: 9 cm.)

(Left) *Genuine graved beaker c. 1800; and* (Right) *Modern faked graving on early beaker.*

Set of miniatures c. 1900 made from the tip end of oxhorns and turned on a lathe alongside a full-size beaker. (Maximum height: 3.7 cm, minimum height: 0.8 cm.)

Nineteenth-century turned oxhorn quill-holder. (Height: 7.6 cm, top diameter: 3.1 cm.)

that the containers did not leak when filled with their liquid assets.

Medicine measures made of transluscent horn were used at the medical centres in the Crimean War. The story is told that many medicine glasses were sent out and arrived smashed or cracked so that the medical profession demanded that horn should be used instead.

Beakers are charming articles to have for display on shelves and furniture for their warmth of colouring, and their variety in size, shape and decoration make them ideal collectors' pieces. They may be found in many antique shops and markets throughout the country.

5
SOUNDING HORNS

Matters of Chiefe Importance are in haste
And for more speed dispatched by the horne
Breton

Instruments of horn were known in ancient Egypt, Mesopotamia, Israel and Greece and are still played today by shepherds in Scandinavia, the Balkans, parts of Spain and the Sudan. Various horn instruments appear to have been used during the Greek and Roman times for fanfares, the volume of sound being dependent upon the effort and efficiency of the blower. The Roman shepherds used a short *cornu* while the longer version was blown for signals and was sometimes curved like the buccina which was not unlike the modern tuba. In the medieval period the horn bugle was used either to sound a warning noise or a signal, the horn being either curved in the shape of a crescent moon or left in its natural form, the hornblower holding it in an upward sweeping direction.

The horn used for musical instruments was primarily derived from animal horns suitable for blowing at the tip end. Among many Tropical peoples the horns often had an additional hole cut in the side. (A beautiful example of a buffalo sounding horn, uncarved except for fine dogtooth cuts at the wide eliptical end was recently on the market in London. The wood–like condition of the horn and the patination indicated a date of *c.* 1800.)

The wide variety of horn instruments in use today is made from a number of materials, but very few from natural horn because of the extremely limited range of sound this produces. Natural horn was used by the French for a fanfare in the first half of the eighteenth century in an opera by André Campra called *Achille et Deidamie*. In the Musical Instrument Museum in West Berlin is the only known surviving example of a gemshorn which is made from the horn of the chamois, part of the antelope family, and known in German as *Gemse* or *Gemsbok*. Jim Furner, from Kent, who makes the modern version of the gemshorn today from any suitable horn, considers it to be a useful addition to any early musical group.

> Its pleasant sounds blend well with strings, and other wind instruments, in accompanying the voice, in full or broken consort. Its evocative tone is unequalled for early Christian music.

Furner also points out that the gemshorn has been well documented from the early part of the sixteenth century having been illustrated in various musical treatises, such as Martin Agricola's *Musica Instrumentalis Deudsch* 1528.

One of the traditional musical instruments used in Wales is thought to be the pibcorn or hornpipe. According to the Welsh Folk Museum its tone was described in the eighteenth century by one who heard the instrument as 'medium between the flute and the clarinet or an indifferent hautbois'. The pibcorns exhibited at the Museum have a double-horned tip joined to paired wooden flutes and a splint backing of wood with a single large wooden mouthpiece.

The sounding horn was a simple expedient for making contact with humans as a warning noise or as a signal. The foghorn is one which immediately springs to mind, and according to a West Countryman, hill farmers made contact with their shepherds in this way until the beginning of this century, which reminds one of the earlier Bainbridge horn.

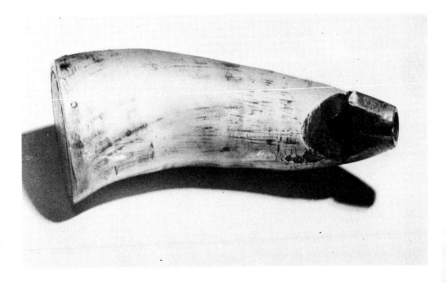

Eighteenth-century white oxhorn sounding horn with wooden bung and iron nails. (Length: 19.5 cm.)

Bainbridge

The warmer climate in England after the final retreat of the great ice sheets from northern Europe allowed great forests of birch and pine trees to spread northwards and these were inhabited by large animals such as the red deer, elk and forest cattle. Groups of hunters also moved northwards and developed methods of hunting and fishing suitable for the lakes and forests. Bow and arrow and barbed spear were the principal means of hunting and fishing. The hunting groups followed the seasonal movements of the deer so that the camp sites in the uplands of the North Yorkshire moors and Pennines were used in the summer months, while during the winter the hunters made use of the lakes and rivers in the lowlands. As the years went by the forests occupying the hills with a mixture of oak, pine and birch provided a source of valuable raw material which was used for trade by the village communities in Wensley Dale, and from this area comes the fascinating story of the Bainbridge forest horn.

Jack Metcalf, who was born in 1899, has since 1947 blown the three blasts on the horn nightly from September 27 to Shrovetide as a traditional remembrance of the times when the area was forested. These blasts told the foresters it was time to bring down their pack-horses laden with cut wood before the winter's night set in. Jack Metcalf has been told that the sound of each twelve seconds' blast may be heard up to three miles away on a clear night, but, as he says, it is something he cannot prove because of the very occupation he has to fulfil.

There are in fact two horns at Bainbridge. The earlier horn, without a mouthpiece, is said to date from the twelfth century, but it is difficult to be very precise without resorting to carbon dating. Until 1977 this horn was kept at Castle Bolton after the arrival in January 1864 of a very beautiful South African oxhorn with brass mounts and chain which was presented to the village by a Mr G. Harburn from Bishop Auckland, Co Durham.

By popular request the older horn was brought back to Bainbridge and both are now housed in the Rose and Crown public house, whose owners patiently accept a never ending stream of requests from visitors to see, feel, and try their prowess on the horn.

No doubt the traditional sounding of the forest horn by the Metcalf family, who have done it for generations, will continue, as Jack Metcalf's great-nephew, Alister, is already very successful in the art of blowing. He is seen in this photograph giving vent on the African horn while his great-uncle is blowing the older oxhorn.

Whistles were used for endless purposes including cycling in

The Metcalfs blowing the Bainbridge horns.

Nineteenth-century antelope whistle.

the nineteenth century as indicated by Hereford Museum and for those who remember the age of the steam train or who have visited the train museum at York there is ample evidence that the movements of trains and people were controlled by the horn whistle. Some have inscriptions along their length giving details of ownership and branch of railway. A fascinating and varied collection may be built up. Some are sold today because of the efficiency of tone. The author knows of one that was purchased for the sole purpose of deterring unwelcome callers on the telephone!

Shofarot

Happy are the people who know the joyful sound.
They walk, O Lord, in the light of Thy Countenance.
Psalm 89, 15.

The word horn in the singular was used to describe the exalted position of a warrior or king, and according to *Cruden's Concordance*:

> This word is often used metaphorically to signify strength and honour, because horns are the chief weapons and ornaments of the animals which possess them; hence they are also used as a type of victory.

The horns were actually worn by individuals in the Middle East to indicate not only a show of strength but also of wealth. Hollowed horns were also used as containers for many purposes, one of the most important being for the consecration of Jewish kings. Samuel took a horn of oil to anoint David and his successor Solomon was anointed by Zadok the priest when he took a horn of oil out of the tabernacle.

The Jews have consistently used horns in religious ceremonies and the most ancient of these, the shofar, is still in use in synagogues today. The shofar is symbollically associated with the story of Abraham's sacrifice of his son Isaac. The instrument was made by heating, flattening and then straightening a ram's horn. The inside would be scraped clean and sometimes surface graving was undertaken. The technique of graving varies considerably in its form, some examples are very crude, the graving is superficial and occasionally a nail or pin has been used which only just cuts into the surface of the horn. It is fairly common to find a shofar with a very precisely carved scallop edge with pierced holes. This is clearly

Shofar found in Leadenhall Street, London, 1855, with no sign of any decoration apart from the patterned cuts at the wide end. Presumed to be of pre-Expulsion period. (Length: 28 cm.)

demonstrated on an example in the Jewish Museum where the graving on the horn states that:

'This ram's horn used in the Jewish Synagogue Sunderland 1860 at the Jewish New Year and the Day of Atonement. The gift of NIS' . . .'

It would seem probable that the inscription quoted above was added by a collector when it was no longer used in the synagogue because of a replacement. No shofar would be likely to have such an inscription while still being used as an instrument during worship. An acceptable practice is to have a quotation in Hebrew from the Psalms.

Today the shofar is only sounded in the synagogues at the New Year, known to the Jews as Rosh Hashanah, and on the Day of Atonement. To quote from the Jewish Museum catalogue:

The Day of Atonement, the tenth day of the month Tishri, the first month of the Jewish year, is the most solemn day of the Jewish Calendar. It concludes the ten Penitential Days which are ushered in by the solemn festival of the New Year. On it, every Jew fasting, both individually and collectively, confesses his sins to God and makes atonement for them to ask forgiveness, by means of repentance, reparation of wrong done to others, and prayer. By this he is deemed to be pardoned and restored to grace. In the service of the synagogue, white vestments replace the mantles of the Law and white curtains are placed in the Ark to symbolize purification. By some, white garments are worn, even by some a white garment resembling a shroud. At the end of the day the shofar, the ancient trumpet made of a plain ram's horn, used in biblical times, is blown and its eerie sound reverberates through the synagogue as a signal that the great Fast is over and that forgiveness is decreed to the repentant.

Mr A. H. Caro of London who was Clerk to the Horners' Company in 1939 and was one of the Sephardic Jews coming as a group from Spain, Italy and Portugal, aptly described the technique used for the sounding of the shofar on these occasions. To quote:

1) *Tekiah* one sustained tone ending abruptly on the fourth or fifth note above the sustained tone. 2) *Shevarim* three groups of two notes each, each making the step of a fourth or fifth. 3) *Teruah* nine very short disconnected staccato notes, or a tremulo on one tone. After the blowing of these three different calls, the Tekiah is repeated. Each of these three calls, regardless

(Above) *Eighteenth-century shofar with scalloped and pierced edge cuts and patterned cuts at the wide end. (Length: 43.1 cm.)*
(Below) *Fine example of shofar dated 1745. The graving in translation from Psalm lxxxi, 4–5: 'Blow the horn on the new moon, at the beginning of the month for our day of festival; for it is a statute for Israel, a decree of the God of Jacob'. (Length: approx. 46 cm.)*

of the number of its tones was considered a unit (one blast). The calls are executed according to this scheme: the group *Tekiah – Shevarim – Teruah – Tekiah* is rendered three times (total twelve calls); then the group *Tekiah – Shevarim – Tekiah* three times (nine calls); and finally *Tekiah – Teruah – Tekiah* three times (nine calls). The sum of these three groups is thirty. This succession of thirty calls is blown three times making a total of ninety calls. To complete the hundred a final group of ten is added in the order 1) *Tekiah – Shevarim – Teruah – Tekiah.* 2) *Tekiah – Shevarim – Tekiah.* 3) *Tekiah – Teruah – Tekiah.* The last *Tekiah* of each of the four sections is prolonged and is called *Tekiah gedelah* the big *Tekiah.*

St. Hubert's Horn

My hoarse-sounding horn
Invites thee to the Chase, the sport of Kings;
Image of war, without its guilt.

Somerville

Nestling on a hilltop of the downs above the village of Idsworth in Hampshire is the beautiful, small chapel of St Hubert which is reached from the roadside by crossing a footbridge over the grass-covered bed of the river which once flowed along the valley. The chapel was built by Earl Godwin and according to records in the Domesday Book, Edward the Confessor held the manor of Idsworth. He would probably have used the chapel during his hunting stays at the manor which was built on lower ground a short distance away. This house still stands today.

Hubert, who was born in AD 656, was the son of Bertrand, Duke of Aquitaine. Hubert married the daughter of Dagobert, Count of Louvain, and was already Bishop of Tongres and Liège when, on Good Friday, AD 683, he was occupied in his favourite pastime of hunting. He was in the forest of Ardennes, when suddenly he was confronted with the vision of a stag bearing a radiant crucifix upright between its antlers. This scene is beautifully depicted in the east window at Idsworth chapel where the oval inset in an otherwise plain glass framing shows Hubert on his knees with arms upraised towards the stag. It is well worth the journey to view the detail and muted colouring of this early work, quite apart from seeing the ancient wall murals, one of which portrays the miracle of Hubert curing a man who believed himself to be a wolf. These murals date from approximately 1300 according to the expert appraisal of Professor Tristram. The mural of Hubert is probably unique.

Following the vision of the stag with the crucifix, Hubert

St Hubert's Chapel, Idsworth. AD *1053.*

Oval inset of stained glass depicting Hubert with arms upraised towards the stag bearing crucifix between its antlers.

renounced his rights to the Duchy of Aquitaine, took holy orders and for a time lived the life of a hermit in the forest. He died in 727 at Tervueren, near Brussels.

There are many beautiful examples of sounding horns which depict the hunt, sometimes showing a pictorial history of St Hubert as in the case of the one held by the Metropolitan Museum of Art in New York. Nothing was known about this hunting horn before its purchase by Horace Walpole in about 1750. In the Strawberry Hill House sale of 1842 it was sold for one hundred and thirty-five guineas and passed through the hands of various people before being acquired from a member of the Rothschild family by Mr and Mrs Martin of New York who have kindly lent it to the museum. Leonardvs Lemovicvs is the artist's signature on this French Renaissance horn made during the reign of François I who was a famed hunter. The natural oxhorn has been covered in four cast sections and has been described as a 'rare Limoge enamel and perfectly unique'.

The horn which is most strongly attributed to St Hubert is in the possession of the Wallace Collection in London. The provenance on this particular horn was largely provided by M Jean Poly of Paris in 1936 who was probably a research agent and employed by J. C. Mann, a medieval specialist and Keeper of the Wallace Collection at that time.

The horn was bought by Sir Richard Wallace in 1879 from Comte de Scey, the descendant of the Seigneurs de Chauvirez, for 15,000 fr. with Charles Yriarte, a well-known writer on art, acting as an intermediary for the purchase.

In 1468, Charles the Bold, Duke of Burgundy had a meeting with Louis XI at Péronne. The duke was immensely angry about the unexpected news of a rising by the Liègois, which was purported to have been stimulated by agents of the king. As a result of this information Charles seized the king and forced him to go with him to Liège to the palace to rescue the Bishop of Liège who was besieged there. Louis de Bourbon, Prince Bishop of Liège, was a relative of the duke and in gratitude for his effective protection from the Liègois, gave Charles the horn of St Hubert which was said to have been preserved among other relics of the saint whom, as we know, had been Bishop of Liège. Charles then built the chapel of St Hubert at Chauvirez-le-Châtel (Haute Saône) and while the altarpiece was carved to show the vision of St Hubert, the horn was hung on one of the pillars. In correspondence, written by Yriarte, he states that before the horn was fixed to the pillar in the chapel, Charles had it enriched with ornamentation of Gothic design, reproducing the architectural features of the chapel. It was also mounted with three bands of silver gilt metal. He goes on to say that this addition altered the primitive character of the horn, but with the chapel it drew many faithful pilgrims who believed that it was a focal point for the cure of hydrophobia.

Presumed seventh-century St Hubert's horn with fifteenth-century additions. (Length: 49.5 cm.)

In 1636 the château was besieged by the French during the Thirty Years' War and the Seigneur de Chauvirez, who was heir to the Duke of Burgundy, fled to Gray, taking the horn with him and entrusting it to the Dames de L'Annonciade, who placed it in their church. It remained in their possession until 1646 when the seigneur asked for the return of the horn and rather unexpectedly the Ursuline nuns refused to part with it. As a result the Parlement de Dôle (Jura) was invoked and the nuns surrendered the horn, but it is believed one silver ring mount was withheld on its return, as originally there were three.

From this time onwards the horn was given a wooden support at its wide end purely to hold it in position and prevent its complete entry into the casing in which it was put for safe keeping in the chapel. This casing made of iron and painted black was probably fashioned by the village blacksmith. The lid with a lock fills the mouth of the iron coiled horn. Attached to it is an iron chain of twelve heavy links, but this chain is a later addition.

There seems little doubt that the fifteenth-century gesso duro almost completely covered the horn in relief when it was first applied. Although it can now be seen with black at the edges there is ample evidence of gilding and blue and grey-green known as amergris on the floral tracery work. Some of the gesso banding, particularly the main central band, shows colouring including amergris, verdigris, gold and wine, varying in its application of colouring order.

The silver gilt metal bands of champlevé design show some verdigris, amergris, and gold and it is interesting to notice that the first band is more detailed, with greater precision and artistry, whereas the second narrow band is altogether more crudely executed.

The horn itself, which is translucent oxhorn of high quality with very little solid tip, has been scored deliberately, presumably to hold the adhesive for the gesso work when it was first applied. The translucency has been reduced by the application on the interior of a greyish green wash. It was a technique used freely by Humpherson of Bewdley, Worcestershire, with the forest horns he made from the eighteenth century, but he chose a terra cotta wash which is characteristic of his hornwork.

St Hubert's horn is fascinating to examine and it is possibly one of the best preserved early horns known to exist, although its fifteenth-century additions have sadly been damaged by the conditions experienced inside the iron casing over a long period of time.

Ripon

The horn, the symbol of legal authority.
Sir Walter Scott

Ripon in North Yorkshire possesses four horns; the first dating from AD 886 was used nightly and also carried through every street in the Liberty at Candlemas, Wednesday of Rogation week, Easter Monday, the Sunday after Lammas, and St Stephen's day. This charter horn was a symbol representing an ancient usage and custom, known to the Saxons and Danes, and was granted instead of a written charter during King Alfred's reign as a form of legal tenure. This freed the Liberty (an area within approximately a ten-mile radius of the cathedral providing a sanctuary from all forms of attack) from royal taxes. It resulted in one of the first forms of local government with the formation of a headman who was given the title of wakeman, with twenty-four assistants and twelve elders. The first wakeman was appointed for life and subsequent appointments were made annually from the elders. The feudal lord was the Archbishop of York. The task of the original wakeman was to keep law and order from nine at night until daybreak. He employed a nightwatchman who set the watch by sounding the horn in the market square three times at nine o'clock. During the course of the night the horn was blown on three separate occasions outside the wakeman's house to show that the duty was being performed. According to the earlier ordinances it was the duty of the wakeman to 'cause a horn to be blown'. This fact is frequently misinterpreted by recorders of the history of the Ripon hornblowing and it is wrongly

The original Ripon horn used from 886–1690.

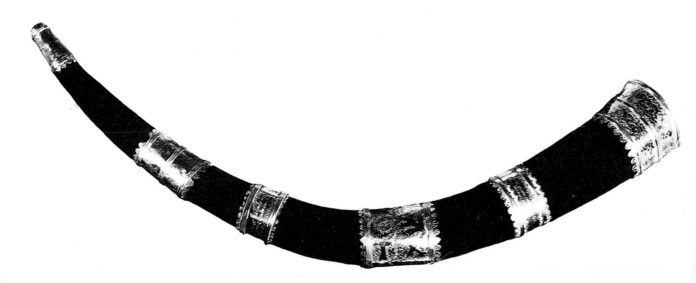

assumed that the wakeman always undertook the job himself. This is highly unlikely as he would not blow the horn on three separate occasions during the night outside his own house 'to show that duty was done'. The town dwellers were forced to pay an early form of insurance policy to the wakeman on the following scale – 'He that hath a gate door and a back door 4d. in the year of duty and of every house-holder having but one door, 2d.' In other words the wakeman was finally responsible during the night for law and order. If by some misfortune a house was broken into, the resident was in a position to try to find the wakeman guilty of negligence. If proven the wakeman had to pay a fine.

As years went by the numbers of the elders and assistants grew and the administration became very unwieldy with many problems. In 1590 the Archbishop of York was approached, but as he was feudal lord he was loath to change the system. Finally, in 1604, Hugh Ripley, the wakeman at that time, approached the King, James I, who drew up a charter and abolished the wakeman, elders and assistants and appointed in their place a mayor (Hugh Ripley), alderman and councillors, with reduced numbers, thus enabling the council to become a more efficient and manageable working body. From this time on constables were appointed to keep law and order so the official job of the wakeman came to an end but the horn carrying and blowing continued for ceremonial purposes. The market cross in Ripon dates from 1598 and it is recorded that from that time the horn would be blown 'at nine in the evening on the four corners of the cross at the Market Stead'. After this ceremony the hornblower went to the Mayor's house and sounded the horn three times on the spot.

In 1686 the mayor, who was also landlord of the White Hart, was robbed and many of the 'antiquities of the town grievously pillaged especially the horn which was robbed of its ancient muniments'. In 1690 the mouthpiece was removed, and the horn was coated in blue velvet and the tip end capped in silver. In 1702 the baldric was produced in its present form and each adornment records the trade or family crest of each wakeman, or from 1604 the mayor; the earliest surviving one is dated 1515 with the name of Thomas Fysscher on the horseshoe.

The original horn is now only taken out when the mayor attends a civic service on Easter Sunday, St Wilfred's Sunday, Battle of Britain day, Remembrance Sunday, Christmas Day, and during the mayor-making ceremony. It is in fact carried by the sergeant at mace because it is considered too heavy for the mayor.

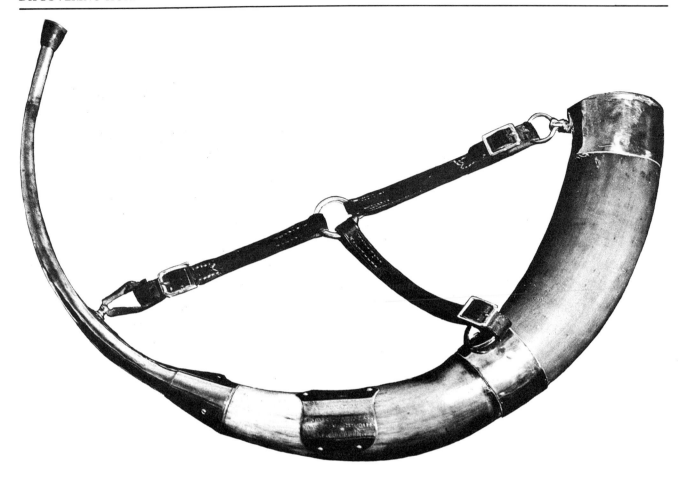

The second Ripon horn used from 1690–1865.

The second horn which is again an oxhorn was bought by the corporation in 1690 for six shillings and eightpence (equivalent today to approximately £12.80), mounted in copper bands with brass rings and leather straps for holding. The tip is mounted in brass with a pewter mouthpiece. It is recorded that the corporation bought this as a standby horn and were outraged at the excessive price.

The second horn was used until 1865 and the date happens to coincide closely with the replacement of the Bainbridge oxhorn. Another interesting connection between the two places is that a man called Jim Horner was photographed blowing the Bainbridge horn in 1864. (He being a kinsman of the Metcalf family.) Ripon has records which show that in 1525 William Horner was wakeman and his family continued to fulfil the job for years with little interruption. Further research

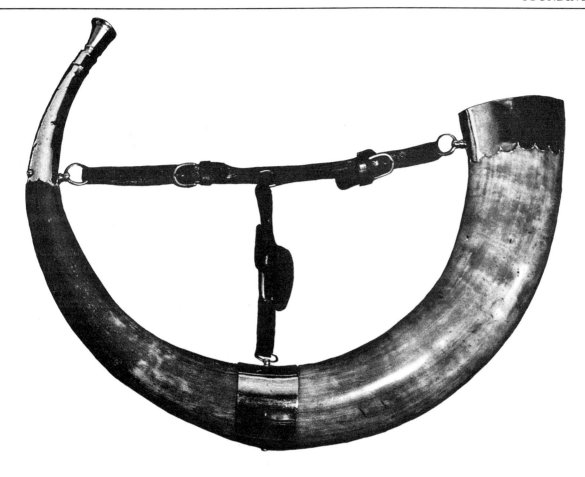

The third Ripon horn used from 1865.

with these families, horns, and places may yield a closer tie than has been previously suspected.

The third horn, presented by Mayor B. P. Ascough, a tallow chandler, is a most beautiful example of South African oxhorn, but like the Bainbridge horn has been wrongly called a buffalo horn. It has magnificent translucent honey toning, has been artificially curved to form a U shape, is banded with brass, and held by leather strapping. It is this horn which is blown today by the hornblower, who is currently paid £1 a night for the ritual, including the wearing of the traditional uniform.

In 1886 the Very Rev W. R. Freemantle, Dean of Ripon Cathedral, presented the corporation with a splendid example of oxhorn, but this, with its adornments, has remained silver capped and is always looked upon as a presentation to record

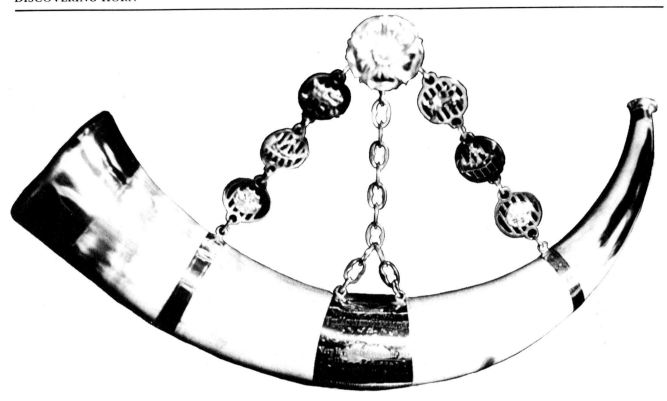

The fourth Ripon horn presented in 1886 and known as the Millenary Horn.

the thousand years of Ripon's existence, so it is known as the Millenary horn.

During the American bicentenary celebrations in 1976, a very well known figure in Ripon, California, called Talbot Kendal, asked John Richmond who, at that time was Mayor of Ripon, Yorkshire, if the Ripon horn could be brought out for the Almond Blossom Festival. Three days later the mayor was on his way to the United States with all his regalia and solid gold chain of office, accompanied by the sergeant at arms and the 1690 horn. The Almond Blossom Festival became quite an historic occasion in California for there were three Ripon mayors present to participate in the festival; one from Ripon, Wisconsin, one from Ripon, California, and one from Ripon, Yorkshire. The horn was duly blown at 9 pm by the sergeant at mace. On this occasion the city tie of Ripon, Yorkshire, was presented as a gift by John Richmond to each of his American counterparts. This presentation was anticipated and planned – the next one was not.

Talbot Kendal, along with other dignitaries, came to see John Richmond off at San Francisco airport – while bidding farewell Talbot Kendal said 'I have two ambitions; one to have a Ripon city tie and the other to have a Ripon horn'. With his usual spontaneity and quick thinking, John Richmond whipped off his city tie and presented it with the comment 'Your first ambition is easy to fulfil, the second is not impossible but will take a little longer!'

In October of the same year John Richmond was on his way back to America with the blessing of Ripon City Council bearing two Chillingham oxhorns which had been prepared by Abbey Hornworks, Kendal, who had arranged for the silver mounts to be added. They are in fact drinking horns and each one was to be presented to the Ripon mayors at a function in Talbot Kendal's house to mark the occasion of the bicentenary gathering earlier in the year. The Mayor of Wisconsin was regrettably unable to be present so the drinking horn was sent to Wisconsin by the Californian people at a later date.

6

HORN ARTEFACTS

Fill me with the best of powder
Ile make your rifle crack the louder.

Powder and Priming horns

Horns were ideal containers for gunpowder, not only for the sportsmen and soldiers, but also for miners and quarrymen. Horns had many attributes, perhaps the main ones being that they were non-flammable, durable, waterproof, easy to fill or empty, often curved to fit against the body for ease of carrying or sometimes flattened to put into a pocket or pouch.

The making of a powder-horn, while keeping its natural shape, was a fairly straightforward task. The core was taken out by natural drying, or boiling with a little potash, and then the solid tip end would either be removed or bored as far as the start of the hollow. The blunted tip end of the horn sheath was then whittled down, leaving a ridge to hold the shoulder cord in place. The horn would then be cleaned, using a scraper along its length. Early powder horns never show the mark of a lathe to do this job, which is therefore a fairly reliable indication of the genuine article as opposed to the fake. Once the cleaning was finished the horn was ready to have a bung inserted at the tip end. This may be made of horn also, sometimes wood or occasionally cork. The can or wide end may be closed. with a variety of materials, including either horn, metal, wood, vellum, leather or sometimes a walnut shell. Hardwood pegs, metal pins, tiny tacks, or brass- or copper-headed nails were used to hold these materials in place. It is sometimes found that the plug is caulked with tallow or perhaps hemp to ensure a perfect fit.

Some of these powder-horns were made from the famous Texas Longhorns which provided a natural greenhorn translucency when scraped. They were ideal as the quantity of contents could be seen when held to the light without resorting to tapping for resonance, or estimating the weight for quantity. The horns only required to be polished and fitted with a shoulder strap of leather or some other suitable material.

Powder-horns have been decorated in an endless variety of ways using the scrimshaw technique. Fruit dyes were sometimes used from the sumac and raspberry for the reds, while carbon black was utilized from the kettle base.

A fine example of an eighteenth-century naval powder-horn was on the market in 1980 with the concave face deeply graved with large lettering 18P^r N3. This type of horn was used by gun-captains on the eighteen-pounder deck of a ship to prime the gunpowder charge through the touch-hole. The 'priming' was ignited by either a lighted slow match or the flintlock. This particular horn will have been used on board a naval vessel of the Red Squadron as the painting depicts a cannon draped with the red ensign. Before 1864 naval vessels flew either the Red, White or Blue ensign dependent upon the Admiral's ranking. A Rear Admiral was first an officer of the Blue, then White and then Red. He would then progress to Vice Admiral of the Blue to White to Red and finally as full Admiral he would rank through the colours again to Red. It is interesting to note that Nelson was Vice Admiral of the White and Collingwood was Vice Admiral of the Blue at the Battle of Trafalgar. After 1864 the White Ensign has always been flown by naval vessels while the Red Ensign has been flown by civilian craft.

Translucent oxhorn powder horn with turned oak cap pinned with iron nails, c. 1680. Tip end closed with horn bung. (Outer curve: 46 cm.)

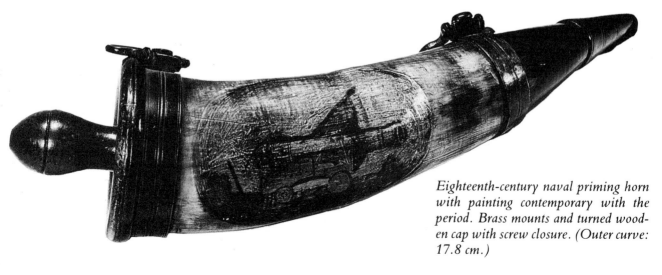

Eighteenth-century naval priming horn with painting contemporary with the period. Brass mounts and turned wooden cap with screw closure. (Outer curve: 17.8 cm.)

57

Eighteenth-century finely graved powder horn with pictorial map of North-Eastern America incorporating Royal Arms of Great Britain and crest of hand grasping two sprigs of olives with motto 'In spirerata florut'. (Outer curve: approx. 31 cm.)

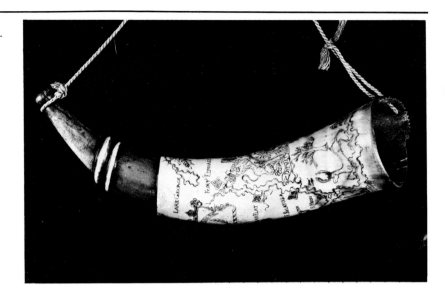

Late seventeenth-century Nordic flat-sided powder horn with gravel floral and geometric designs, inscribed ESPE-GAARD. (Outer curve: 17.8 cm.)

Another interesting feature in this painting is the bar-shot below the cannon. A similar form with a cannon ball at either end of a chain is known as chain-shot. Collectively they are known as 'dismantling shot' as they were used to damage enemy rigging.

Powder- and priming-horns have provided their owners with a natural 'canvas' which has been well utilized. They incorporate geographical, historical, pictorial and sporting scenes. The quality of graving varies considerably and this must be taken into consideration when the purchase of a decorated one is being contemplated. It is very difficult to establish beyond doubt whether many of the American graved powder-horns were used as necessary pieces of equipment or whether they were painstakingly graved as souvenirs of past events. There is no doubt that there was plenty of raw material on the spot, for the troops took livestock with them which were slaughtered as needed. Only during really hard, wintry conditions when feeding animals became a problem would there be a major slaughter resulting in a plentiful supply of 'ready to work canvas'. Nevertheless, they provide a fascinating and wide collection of the type of equipment carried by the infantry of the seventeenth and eighteenth centuries.

In order to make a flattened powder-horn it is better to let the horn 'season' for up to a year before heating it and pressing it to shape. It is far less likely to resort to its original shape if this precaution is taken. Many flat powder-horns have engravings, while others may be stained or dyed. Again the quality of

workmanship must be looked at critically for the staining techniques may be very crudely executed. One particular horn examined was described as being 'of rare quality and colour'. It did not actually specify the quality but the price tag indicated the esteem with which it was held!

Stag and oxhorns were the most commonly used type, certainly for the decorated versions, but examples of buffalo are not unknown, although it is a much heavier horn and more difficult to handle. The Tower of London has a fascinating collection of graved powder-horns from many European countries. Among them is a group of five very fine German powder-horns dating from the sixteenth-century, each made from stag antler beams incorporating the fork of the first pair of tines; the outer face of the horn in each case is engraved with human figures with a background of foliage and the mountings are of steel with a belt hook.

The Tower also has a Norwegian oxhorn powder-horn dating from c. 1700. To quote:

> The graving shows horizontal bands of human figures, some mounted and including Adam and Eve with the Tree of Knowledge, David and Charlemagne, their names inscribed beside them. The bands of figures are separated by inscriptions:

> FERAKVND – HABAROLAFSTRANGSNON –
> TALAGMASSONEGENHAI

> The writing is a collection of names from the Nordic legends, i.e. Habar, Olaf Strangsnon; the second is the signature of the maker, Talag Massön, followed by Egen Hai, i.e. by his own hand.

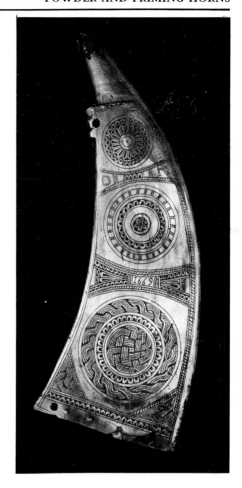

Dated 1669, flat-sided powder horn with finely executed geometric and interlacing work. Reverse side has cruder work within panels, a not uncommon feature on early powder horns. (Length: approx. 30 cm.)

Dark oxhorn powder horn with fine quality silverwork. Inside flower on butt end plate is silversmith's mark GS (George Scott admitted 1677). Slide opening at wide end and silver pin with chain attachment at the tip end. (Approx. length: 15.4 cm.)

59

AD *7–8th century Scandinavian spindle whorl showing geometric roundel work. (Diameter: 3.8 cm.)*

(Right) Seventeenth-century ram's horn priming horn with northern European type graving in roundel and geometric design with hand-forged iron and brass work. The ends of the horn are closed with wood. (Height: 21.4 cm.)

The Worshipful Company of Horners has a lovely example of a powder-horn. It is probably made from a section of a ram's horn. The flask has a rich, mellow brown toning, very similar to seventeenth-century quality oak. The concentric pin gravings and roundels, of the Scandinavian type, are finely executed on the smooth side of the horn, while the classical ridging remains undecorated on the opposite side. It has been documented as being buffalo horn which may be understood because of the ridging, but the colouring and the texture suggested closer examination. The base and top are of wood which has been fitted into place with hand-made iron nails. The metalwork is of iron and the general impression from an arms' specialist would be that this is a rare early piece from the seventeenth century. The photograph of the Scandinavian spindle whorl dating from the seventh to eighth centuries AD shows very similar roundel work which is typical of the northern European graver, although it must be remembered that this style could be, and was, copied by others as a result of the trading between countries. (*See* page 60.)

Brass mounted oxhorn priming flask in fine condition, c. 1800. (Outer curve: 19.5 cm.)

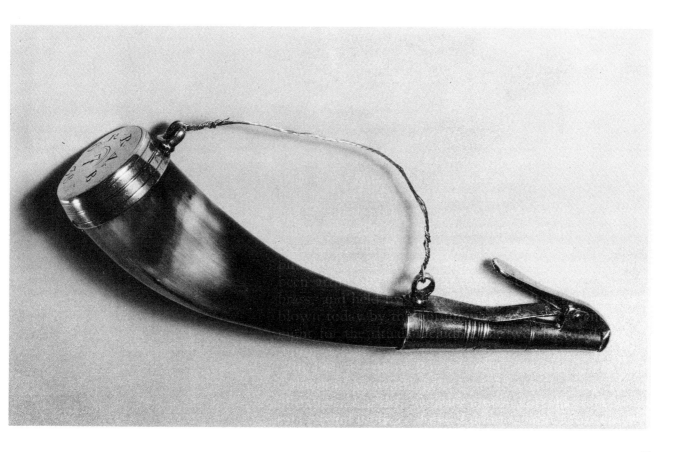

Shoe horns

Shoe horn engraved with floral and geometric designs dated 1595 and inscribed THIS IS RICHARD CRABS SHOE IN HORNE MADE BY THE HAND OF ROBART MINDVM. *(Length: approx. 20.3 cm.)*

The shoe horn is probably one of the most practical items of everyday usage. Most households possess one and they come in a multitude of shades, colours, lengths and styles.

Shoe horns are the subject of ardent graving by the craftsman Robart Mindum, whose work covers the period between 1593–1612, and these make valuable collectors' items. York Castle Museum has a shoe horn very similar to the type illustrated, but lacks the more usual addition of Mindum's name. In each case the graving follows both floral and geometric designs with the lettering clearly defined and spaced.

The examples of the Mindum shoe horns which have been examined were made from white oxhorn which has mellowed with age and acquired a patina which would be difficult to fake. Some of them have an almost tawny shading although the letterings and gravings retain their original stains which bring out the detail so well.

The age old process of making these shoe horns is continued today with little alteration in the technique other than the labour-saving use of electricity and the addition of some commercially prepared polishes. The horner selects a suitable length of oxhorn which is then cut in two along its natural curve by a bandsaw. This process which seems so simple requires in fact considerable skill, for if the horn is cut wrongly in the initial stages the fault cannot be rectified. It is then heated until pliable over a flame before being set in a shaped former and pressed in a vice until cool. After being removed, the horner smoothes off the rough edges of the horn and cleans and perfects the shape before subjecting it to three stages of polishing. The final result is a very useful, hard wearing, long lasting item.

There are many shoe horns to be found in antique shops today. The quality and age vary considerably, but they remain very practical items besides forming a highly decorative wall display, particularly if careful selection is made so that a variety of tonings of the horn may be shown; some have very beautiful markings and the earlier ones offer the collector fine examples of patination.

Combs and Backcombs

We there did espy a fair pretty maid,
With a comb and a glass in her hand.
Anon

Combs of one form or another have been in use from very early times, but recorded specimens of these are found in many materials other than horn. In this country the original charter of the Livery Company of Combmakers is dated 1635. Prior to that date it was incorporated with hornworkers in general until the demand justified an independent body. Dating from this period are two very beautifully worked combs in the possession of the Worshipful Company of Horners. They are made from plates of translucent oxhorn and the elaborately pierced designs were probably cut by small ribbon saws, using the same technique as fanstick piercing (*see* section on 'Fans').

There were a number of areas where the horn comb industry flourished, particularly in the seventeenth, eighteenth and nineteenth centuries. The ones mentioned most frequently in books and articles are Aberdeen, Bewdley, Dublin, Kendal, Kenilworth, Milnthorpe, Sheffield and York. The Aberdeen Combworks alone employed more than six hundred people in the middle of the nineteenth century and produced over nine million combs a year in nearly two thousand different varieties. These gargantuan amounts can largely be accounted for by the decorative hair dressing of the women of the time.

One of the very few combmakers' workshops to survive for posterity is the one started by Joseph Rougier in 1794. It is preserved in the cells at York Castle Museum and is a reconstruction of his premises on the site where Rougier Street now runs. As the name implies, the street was named after the great combmaker, the original name having been Tanner Row.

Seventeenth-century translucent oxhorn comb with elaborate pierced designs and individually cut teeth with pearl drop ends. (14×10 cm.)

At its peak the Rougier industry included not only combs but ointment and soap making, which were known to contain the powdered horncore. Subsequently other items were made by the firm from horn including snuff boxes, card cases, buttons, shoehorns, horn scoops, drinking horns and powder flasks.

In the early days combs were a very laborious business to make from horn. In the first place the section of horn was cut, heated and sawn down one side, reheated and flattened into a plate by a vice. When thoroughly cooled the plate would be cleaned and smoothed before being given to the horner who cut the teeth with a hand saw by fastening the intended back of the comb into the clamp which held the horn. The teeth were cut individually with a double-edged saw which left the horn rough on all the cut edges. After this process the comb was subjected to various stages of filing known as grailing which included the tip edge of each tooth and finally the stages of polishing were applied, making use of rottenstone and oil and leather buffing.

A number of metal templates in the Rougier workshops illustrate that many decorative combs were made by embossing them in heated dies and the simpler form of pierced work was accomplished in the same manner.

Inside one of the inventories of the late W. P. Dobson of Milnthorpe was found a sketch of a decorative backcomb.

Seventeenth-century translucent oxhorn comb with finely pierced designs of animals. (14.5×8.5 cm.)

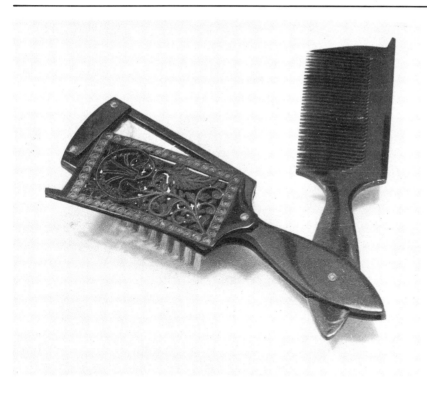

Nineteenth-century buffalo-horn brush and comb travelling-set with pierced work on the hinged covering for the mirror.

Presumably this was the beginnings of a design for a template although no examples are known to have survived from his family's various workshops.

Dobson also prepared the combs and comb-cases for Gould-thorp of Sheffield and again from the Dobson firm's inventories of 1818 it may be seen that pressed work was undertaken by him. These include hunting scenes, birds, Mars, Venus, Freemason's Arms, Washington, cossacks, and the device 'peace and plenty', which were added to various prepared comb-cases before being sent to Gouldthorp who presumably then mounted the combs in the cases on a metal pivot hinge before offering them for sale. Gouldthorp is mentioned by Wilmot Talor in his book *The Sheffield Horn Industry* as one of the prolific horn-pressers. But perhaps it would be more accurate to suggest that he was a die-sinker and that like many of the cutlers, he sub-contracted for his scales and handles although he is listed both as a combmaker at 54 Burgess Street in 1818 and also as a haft and scale-presser and cutter. There is also mention of prepared combs and comb-cases with the impression of Wellington, another of flowers and the staghunts being sent to Fisher (another Sheffield worker) from Dobson. Another is listed as the arms of the United States of America but the name Fisher has been deleted. Similar examples of

(Above) *Nineteenth-century stained oxhorn backcomb with metal hinge on which the gilt metal is mounted to hold the diamante in position.* (Below) *Pierced translucent oxhorn backcomb carefully stained to simulate tortoise-shell.*

these are described within the section of horn-handles and scales.

According to the *Book of English Trades and Library of the Useful Arts* published in 1824, a Mr Bundy from Camden Town had designed and obtained a patent for a machine about ten years' previously, which could cut combs by a twinning process, 'so called because it cut the teeth of two combs at one operation from one piece of material', which naturally speeded up the work considerably. However, documents and articles held by Aberdeen City Libraries state that a Mr Lynn in 1828 invented an identical process of twinning which was incorporated into the flourishing and extensive combmaking factory owned by S. R. Stewart & Co, called The Aberdeen Comb Works. It would be interesting to establish the true and original inventor. Certainly the name of Mr Bundy crops up in records some years before that of Mr Lynn.

In the 1840s and 1850s hair styles had become very elaborate so that the decorative use of backcombs in a variety of designs became popular. As the century crept on hair styles changed frequently, but some form of adornment was used to glamorize the functions of the basic necessity of the comb. The arched comb-head in a variety of forms, either fixed or hinged, was used amongst others throughout this period. Horn was frequently adapted, sometimes carefully stained to simulate tortoiseshell, but the method of decorative mounting should give the identification of materials. Glue would have been used to hold any inset gems in horn, whereas natural contraction upon cooling would have held the gems in tortoiseshell.

Translucent horn was designed in the shapes of bees, dragonflies, birds and flowers during the Art Nouveau period for mountings for brooches, combs and pendants. Sometimes these are found carved and in other instances pressed from moulds. The makers' desire to copy tortoiseshell must always be remembered by the would-be purchaser of any of these articles, but the quality of mounting should be a guide; the quality of workmanship is not. The purchase price should reflect the material used, but at the present time many people are not clear about what is stained horn and what is tortoise-shell.

It was in the 1920s that the slump in the horn comb trade came. The 'bob-cut' during the war had appreciably reduced the demand for fashion combs and the number of those skilled in the trade had retired or died without replacement. In 1931 when the Rougier Works finally closed there were only five staff as a total, one of whom was a combmaker and another was a toothcutter.

Horn combs are still manufactured today by firms in England and Scotland and on the Continent because the demand for an attractive, hard-wearing horn comb still remains.

There is a revival in the interest of dressing combs for the hair, and one firm in Paris is manufacturing various styles which are on the market in some of the large London stores. If a collector or dealer is making a purchase, the surface gloss and finish of these newer horn and simulated tortoiseshell combs should give a clue to the age of the article, for the sheen is highly reflective. The older combs have a softer, mellower touch and the mirror-like polish is missing.

Who goeth a borrowing
Goeth a sorrowing.
Few lend (but fools)
Their working tools.
Tusser

Horn tools and equipment

OXHORN SLIP-TRAILER

Peter Brears, in his book *The English Country Pottery*, discusses the use of a slip-trailer by the potter, and so does Professor Church in his chapter on slip-ware in *Some Minor Arts*. The technique is used for controlling the amount of liquid clay being added for ornament on to the surface of the ware. Various colours were mixed and held in their respective containers. From these the flow could be regulated by means of a quill fitted into the tip of the vessel and a separate air vent controlled by the finger.

The oxhorn is a natural reservoir for this purpose and the angle at which the horn is held controls the speed of the flow, so a cut in the air supply is not necessary and the potter is free to put the horn in a rest until it is required again. A slip-trailer horn was very simple to make. Once cleaned after being boiled it would have the solid top removed to the point of the pencil hole thickness where the core had been. This could be widened with a drill before the quill was fitted into this opening, if necessary, filling in any gaps between the two surfaces with a sealing material such as clay. The younger the horn used, the less amount of solid tip there would be, but equally the size of the reservoir would be reduced, so the potter made his selection depending on the amount of slip he may have wished to use at any given time.

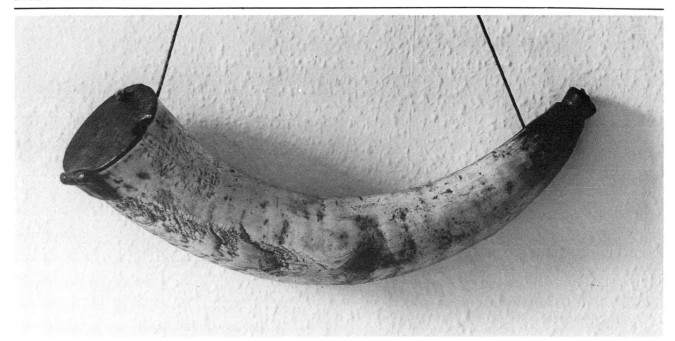

(Above) *Eighteenth-century grease and sanding horn with iron hinge and lid and having a bung approx. 7.8 cm inside the wide end to act as a division for carrying the grease. (Outer edge: 38 cm.)* (Below) *Combined grease and sand-horn typical of the design used in Wales and the Border country. A metal plate is used for closure.*

GREASE- AND SAND-HORNS

An oxhorn is an ideal container for carrying many materials, grease being a very common example. Some are somewhat basic and were used by farmers as a very necessary piece of maintenance equipment for their wagons and other farm vehicles. Others may have some writing graved, or, as the example above shows, there may be a pictorial graving. This particular one has a division at its can, or wide end, so that both sand and grease could be transported simultaneously, although kept separate. This was a fairly popular technique and in some crudely made pieces the sand is carried in the longer section with a thick piece of string attaching it to a shorter piece of horn in which the grease was kept, each of the open ends being closed with a flat plate fitted into a cut slot in the horn. This plate may be made of leather, metal, wood, or horn. St Fagan's has a number of fine examples. Hereford City Museum has an example which shows that the grease and sand were mixed at the outset, but the closing technique remains the same.

The manual worker in mowing or hedge-cutting would always carry a strickle or whetstone as it was vital to have a sharp-edged tool. Naturally the whetstone would be of little use without a mixture of sand and tallow first being smeared across its surface and so the horn was frequently used. Professor Grancsay mentions oxhorn being used in the United

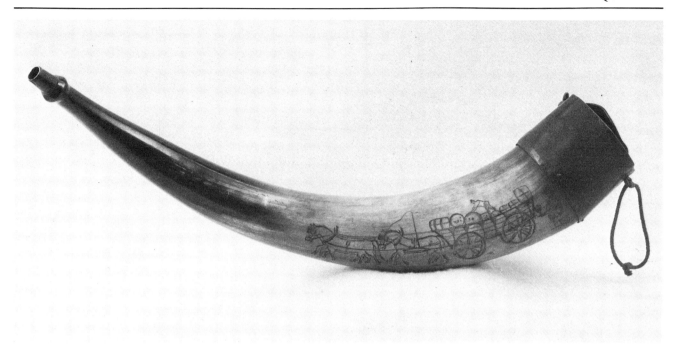

Eighteenth-century grease and sandhorn with pewter band and cap.

States by mowers for carrying the whetstone with vinegar for sharpening scythes. As horn is non-porous, this would be very feasible, although care would have had to be taken to ensure nothing sharp came in contact with the edges of the horn, because it would split and the vinegar would quickly create further damage. If the horn split when grease was being used, this would act as a waterproof seal.

Many of these grease-horns were carried by stage coaches, carriages, and farm carts, as the axles would require greasing at regular intervals. The sand was used to give a better grip when the brake was applied.

SEED SOWER AND STORER

This is such a simple device that it is surprising the horn is not used far more frequently for this purpose today, rather than the paper packets in which the seeds are bought and afterwards stored in for future use. It is a well-known fact that a horn provided with suitable stoppers will keep its contents perfectly dry. The size of the horn may be determined by the user, and the opening at the tip end could be varied with different funnels – either by using quills of varying thicknesses or another suitable substance like a plastic straw. Thus one horn could act as a seed distributor while others could remain for storage.

The technique is very similar to that of the slip-trailer

Eighteenth-century oxhorn seed sower with cork bung. (Outer edge: 17.2 cm.)

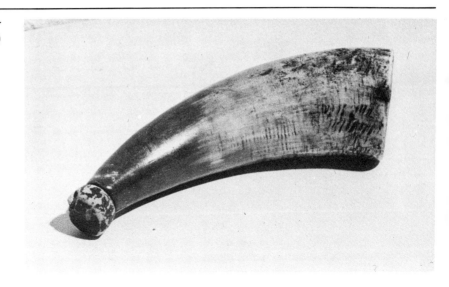

Nineteenth-century hammer made from solid tip of oxhorn drilled to take the beech handle. (Length: 14 cm.)

reservoir. The seed would be sown in regular amounts where required, as opposed to the somewhat jerky action when sown directly from the hand or packet.

HAMMER HEADS

Horn tips were frequently used for hammer–heads since the very shape was ready to be fixed on to a wooden hand grip. The illustrated example shows a solid tip of oxhorn through which a hole has been drilled to take the beech handle. This was a very cheap method of making a reliable and necessary tool. Refined examples of horn hammer heads are used by many silversmiths as the horn proves a softer material to work the various metals.

DRENCHING-HORNS

This method of administering a medicinal draught to an animal provides a simple and straightforward procedure. The horn acts as an excellent container for the liquid, and it makes a natural funnel for the contents to be poured where required. The wide end of the horn would be cut at an angle so that the liquid could be seen as it was poured; the speed of the flow being controlled by the sharpness of the tilt. The horn, being a non-porous structure, could be cleaned easily and used for many different liquids and substances.

It is possible to confuse a drenching-horn with a grease-horn except for the angle of the cut, but on closer inspection it may also be found that the grease-horn will have a more velvety, smooth touch on the inside due to the contents it has carried, and there may be a deepening of colour because of the constant feeding with grease. However, one farmer assured the writer that the drenching horns on his estate were only used for giving doses of castor oil! No doubt the inside of both the horn and animal maintained a pristine appearance! More commonly the dose was linseed oil, which leaves the horn slightly tacky. Monty Ball, a blacksmith in the Bristol area, whose family have plied the trade for some two hundred years, makes a 'brew' of melted lard with salt to treat one of his animals and this is a mixture also known to the head coachman, Ivor Morris, at Ashton Court, Bristol, who looks after the Lord Mayor's horses.

Judging the outside condition of the horn would be useless on the more crudely made ones, as many may not have even had the outside scaling of the horn removed. Many people used them as purely functional items and it was only when time or finances permitted it that the horns were cleaned and engraved. The dating of these horns may be deduced by the 'feel' of the horn, which becomes more woodlike as it ages. As functional items that fulfilled a real need they are interesting to own.

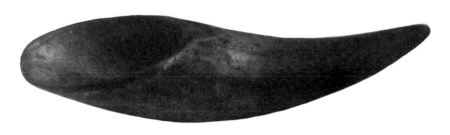

(Left) *A small drenching horn, c. 1800. (Outer curve: 16.5 cm.)* (Below) *Nineteenth-century drenching horn used also as a tongue depressor for animals.*

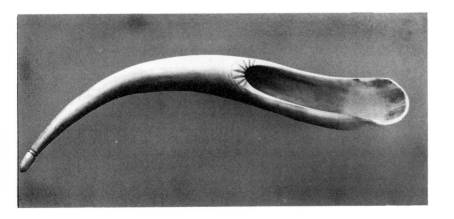

THUMB GUARDS

Thumb guards were made by cutting the tip end off a small oxhorn and then shaping the wider end to fit over the thumb and its surrounding tissues as far as the wrist. These guards were an admirable protection from the sharp instrument used for tree-barking. Tree-barking was traditionally undertaken by women and the work was generally carried out in May when the spring-felled timber was stripped of its bark. After it had been dried on racks, the bark would be carried on carts to the local tanneries where it was used in the production of leather. The staghorn handles of knives and other flatware were frequently subjected to the tanpits to add colour interest to the tines before being fitted with a steel tang.

It would seem very possible for this thumb guard method of protection to be adapted by the hornworkers on the polishing buffs today, instead of using the somewhat flimsy, felt guards made with adhesive strapping which were seen at one factory. But having put forward this suggestion the writer was told the thickness of the horn thumb guard would prevent the user from judging what stage of polished surface the horn had reached. Having the 'feel' of the horn as well as the visual image is clearly an important factor.

Nineteenth-century oxhorn thumb guard used as a protection during tree-barking.

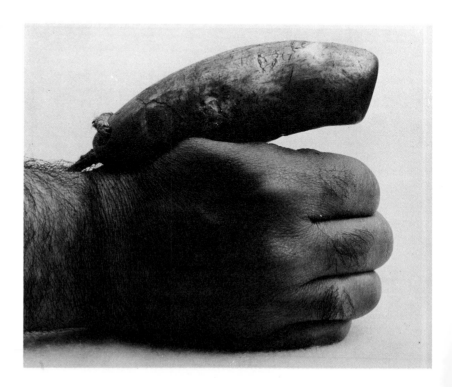

Consular watches and Pair cases

See how the moments pa*l*s,
How swift they haste away
In this instructive gla*l*s
Behold! Thy Life's decay.
Waste not then thy prime
In sins' pernicious road,
Redeem thy precious tyme,
Acquaint thyself with God.
So when thy pulse shall cease
Its throbing transient play,
Thy soul to realms of peace
Shall wing its joyful way.
The Watch's Memento

There are many examples of consular watches and pair-cases made from horn in museums, private collections, and a few become available on the market for the interested purchaser. It is not proposed to discuss the working of the watch in any way at all. This very specialist subject is well covered by authoritative works including especially the new edition of *Antique Watches* by Camerer Cuss, published in 1976. There is, however, relatively little information on the casings made from horn.

By definition a consular watch is one which has only a single case which opens and the spring will release the watch itself. A pair-case watch is one which has both an outer and an inner casing. The inner casing was often very decoratively pierced with the outer covering acting as a protection and therefore underpainted to add interest. Watch-paper was frequently used between the inner and outer casings to prevent any movement between the two surfaces, thus acting as a washer to take up any slack. As Cedric Jagger told the writer, these papers often carried the details of the maker, sometimes that of the repairer, and frequently there were charming verses included like the one quoted (with its original spelling) at the beginning of this section, which is 'housed' inside a pair case exhibited in the Clock Room, Guildhall Library.

Most people liked pretty watches and the functional side of the watch sometimes suffered in favour of the decoration. The majority of hornwork for watches is found on pieces dating towards the second half of the eighteenth century. Very thin horn, like tortoiseshell, is susceptible to fracture and it is rare to find an example which does not have a crack or perhaps a replacement repair. There are wide variations in the standard of metal workmanship on the horn casings which are usually in gilt metal frames with gilt metal tooling, and it is generally said

1790 consular case of underpainted horn depicting the Clockmakers' Arms from the Royal Charter of 1631.

1765 pair case of underpainted horn in muted shades of green, gold and red with black fernwork. The central figure depicts a woman leaning against an upright anchor.

73

(Above) *Late eighteenth-century pair case of underpainted horn. The central portion depicts a seated woman holding a book with her right arm resting on a monument.* (Centre) *Late eighteenth-century consular case of underpainted horn depicting an officer with a young girl in foreground with a background of soldiers in a firing line.* (Below) *Late eighteenth-century consular case of underpainted horn.*

'poor watch, poor horn'. In other words, if the quality of the watch itself did not merit an expensive covering material, then a very cheap expedient, like horn, was used. Today the skill of the artist who used this medium may now be enjoyed by the collector. Some of the colourings are exquisite in muted shades of green, gold, red, blue, and black. The fineness of the detail deserves examination with a magnifying glass to pick out the care and precision with which some of the underhorn painting was done. The cases with pictorial designs were often copied from a picture, varying only in some of the details. Fern decoration is a very common feature on horn cases, and this work is usually depicted in black.

Some horn cases have been subjected to tortoiseshell markings in a variety of greens, blues, browns and even black. Here again the collector needs to tread with care. The casing may have been underpainted with vermilion and a brownish black giving the impression of tortoiseshell. When compared with the genuine article a variety of 'ingredients' is missing. The rich lustre of tortoiseshell; the water-marking as described in the section on dyeing and staining; the use of gilt metal instead of gold for the framework and it will also be noticed that the punched tool-work markings on the nail heads are less sharp and defined because of the harder metal. On fine examples of watches which have gold or silver pinning, the punching of the tooled nail shows a sharper impression because of the softer metal. Providing tortoiseshell prices are not paid for these examples of underpainted horn cases, they make a fascinating collection of dye colours depicted on translucent horn which in itself has undergone hours of preparation by the horner.

Remembering that oxhorn has quite a variety of tonings, do not lose sight of the fact that this could be and was incorporated into articles in its natural polished state. Such horn is again used on border casing work on watches and frequently wrongly described as being tortoiseshell. The author has examined a number of watches where this has been inaccurately attributed.

Metal inlay work was undertaken extensively in Sheffield where the design often included animals like squirrels, birds, and rabbits, as well as flowers and scroll work. Similar designs are sometimes found on the outer casings of pair-cases with either natural oxhorn or simulated tortoiseshell being used. Inlay and piqué work on horn required to be glued as contraction of the horn would not be enough to keep the added work in place. In spite of this precaution some inlay is often missing, but it does not detract from the generally pleasing appearance of the article. It is very often assumed that inlay and piqué work was only undertaken on tortoiseshell because the similarity and treatment of oxhorn is not always appreciated.

Consular watches and pair-cases using horn give a fairly extensive insight to the horn collector. They not only show the ingenuity of the horner with his technical knowledge required for making the horn transparent in some cases, but they also show clearly the variety and artistic application required for the dyeing, the painting, and the piqué work on to this natural and versatile material.

> Great light a lanthorne made of horne doth cast,
> Which with a candle in dark night is borne.
>
> *Breton*

A particularly interesting use of horn was as a transparent shield to prevent air currents from causing variations in the burning of the time candle. The Romans had horn window panes and the lights were made from the hollow portion of oxhorn. Lanthorn continued in use until the middle of the nineteenth century for window lights and some old house inventories have them listed as individual items because of their worth.

Horn was also used for lanthorn leaves There are a number of these lanterns in existence today which may be seen in museums, on HMS *Victory* in the surgeon's quarters, in private country houses, and occasionally they may be bought on the open market. The early ones were narrower than the later ones, often with only the hinged section containing a lanthorn leaf as may be seen in the Museum of London where there is one dating from the eighteenth century. Other examples have lanthorn leaves all the way round set in a metal frame of either brass or tin. The shapes of these lanterns are various and include square, triangular, and round. Museums, especially York Castle Museum, have a number on display in the furnishings of the early kitchens, while Aberdeen Museum has one hanging in a most characteristic setting above the stairway in Provost Skene's house. Perhaps one of the most enchanting is in the possession of the Pitt Rivers Museum in Oxford. It is a beautifully preserved example of diminutive size dating from the seventeenth century and reputed to have been used by ladies under their cloaks after lights had been extinguished!

Throughout the nineteenth century Humpherson had a flourishing horn factory at Bewdley where, according to records kindly supplied by Stephen Price, an enormous number of lanthorn leaves were prepared, the frames for

Lanterns

Seventeenth-century metalwork lantern having lanthorn leaves set in the open framework. (Maximum height: 17.2 cm, diameter: 6.4 cm.)

75

Nineteenth-century metalwork lantern with original lanthorn leaves. (Height: 45 cm.)

which came from a local source and from metalworks in Wolverhampton.

The lanthorn leaves were made from the central portion of oxhorn, first heated, split and flattened under pressure. As horn is stratified a short round-nosed knife called a lift was inserted in the edge of the horn and plates or leaves raised. This technique is being experimented with by hornworkers today, but the results have so far been disappointing. Extreme thinness made for transparency, a quality which was produced by subjecting the leaf to a heated vice, previously coated with tallow, before being scraped further and polished. The leaf was easily made malleable again by heating in boiling water in order to curve it to the shape of a lantern frame. It was then held in position with the required metal clips at the opening within the frame. Horn is of course a non-flammable natural product which makes it an ideal material for use with lighting in this form.

There is a lantern dating from 1850 which has been painted over with gold, hanging in the baptistry of Chester Cathedral. This has been adapted for use today by wiring the lantern for electricity. Sadly some of the lanthorn leaves have been replaced with pale green glass. Perhaps conservationists could restore this correctly as it is a very well-preserved, decorative example of its type.

Lanterns were a fairly commonplace item in the home and were of course used as a method of carrying sheltered light whether the user was on foot or using transport. Because of the safety factor and the ever-rising cost of electricity they may again become welcome articles within the home as a charming form of soft lighting, quite apart from the fun of using them at Christmas for carol singing and for parties.

Mid nineteenth-century copper base, metal lantern used by a child when going to school. Two restored lanthorn leaves. (Maximum height: 15.8 cm, diameter: 5.6 cm.)

Here she comes i'faith full sail, with her fan spread and streamers out, and a shoal of fools for tenders!

Congreve

Fans

Horn fans which were made in quantity from the Regency period to the end of William IV's reign were very fashionable in England and there are many pretty examples.

The fan sticks were frequently made with transparent oxhorn, the shape being determined by a specially formed cutter. Subsequently, the fan sticks could be stained to add variety and colour, or as a deliberate intention to fake tortoise-

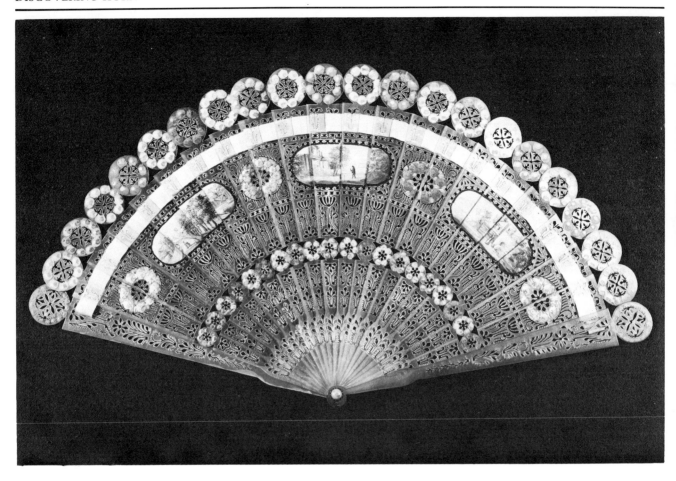

Finely pierced translucent oxhorn brisé fan. Dutch. First quarter nineteenth century.

shell. Like the watch–cases made of horn, the necessary metal-work is the best detector of its true origin. If the metal rivets and hanging loop are made of brass the answer is most probably horn, not tortoiseshell. Also, the silver metal piqué work on horn requires to be held by glue because the contraction when the horn cools is not sufficient to hold the decoration in place. With tortoiseshell this is not the case and the fan worker would probably use real silver or gold anyway since his shell had been expensive to buy initially.

The transparent brisé fans, made of extremely thin sticks of horn, are pierced by means of a wire with the thickness of a watch spring which is fed into a tiny saw. The result of this work is quite fairy-like on the better examples and although very flexible to handle the fans themselves are quite tough. These are often found in perfect condition apart from the ribbon, the replacing of which is described in Nancy Armstrong's book *A Collectors' History of Fans.*

Many of these fans are decorated with tiny flowers – violets, roses, forget-me-knots, and tulips – which will sometimes be predominantly of one colour on the front with an alternative predominance on the back.

Sometimes the fan sticks are comparatively thick, although still pierced, and they may be mounted with a paper fan held in place with gilt metal thread. The one illustrated is signed Maleu and the pictures are clear with a wealth of soft colouring.

Horn fans may be found in many shapes including the cockade fan in translucent filigree work. There is often no additional use of colour and the quizzing glass in the centre is frequently held in place by a brass ring mount.

Another interesting example is the Sumatran fan with a translucent oxhorn plaited handle with a skeleton frame of horn holding the vellum in place with overstitching in linen thread. The pierced vellum is usually adorned with a tradi-

Nineteenth-century translucent oxhorn brisé fan painted with roses, lilac and forget-me-nots. Regency period.

Nineteenth-century fan with thick horn pierced sticks mounted with a paper fan incorporating landscapes with figures and buildings. Signed Maleu.

tional Wayang, 'being' shadow-puppet figure. These fans are often described as being made of buffalo horn, but it is unlikely since buffalo is a heavier horn, more brittle and difficult to mould and almost impossible to make translucent.

It is surprising that fans like the ones described have not been mounted in a type of picture frame so that they may be enjoyed as a permanent display while protecting them from both damage and dust. Dust is very apt to collect in the pierced areas of these fans, but no moisture of any sort should be used to clean them because the damp could be absorbed by the edges of the piercing which would cause splitting of the laminated surfaces. A piece of really soft, dry chamois leather used with a slight amount of pressure while the fan is resting on a flat surface is probably all that will be necessary. Otherwise the painstaking job of using a long fine hair paint brush will clear the tiny crevices.

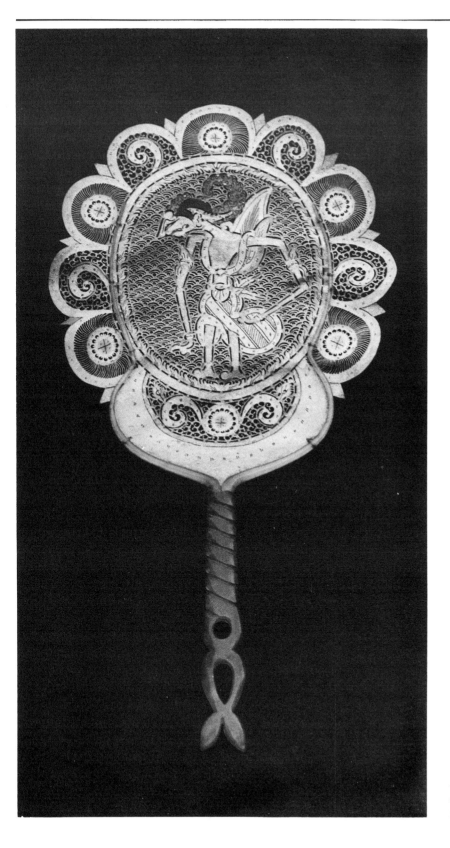

Nineteenth-century Sumatran fan with oxhorn handle and skeleton frame holding vellum in place.

Brooches

I will make you brooches and toys for your delight.
R. L. Stevenson

Brooches in horn date from the second half of the nineteenth century and there are many examples to be seen in both private collections and antique shops today. Too often they are labelled incorrectly as being tortoiseshell, merely because the craftsman has chosen and worked his horn carefully. The basic shapes chosen by the horner when using either gold or silver piqué work tend to be round, oblong or hexagonal. Some of this charming work comes from either the Birmingham or Sheffield area where so much of a similar type of work was undertaken at one time. Most of these brooches with piqué work have a hollow back and perhaps here again the guide to horn is given by the thickness of the material. Tortoiseshell brooches tend to be much thinner so that the tonings may be seen with much greater ease. The other guide between the two materials is that gold pins and hinges were used for tortoiseshell since it was such an expensive commodity in the first place, whereas generally with horn examples pins and hinges were made from brass or steel.

The piqué work in Sheffield was first undertaken by a French expert in the town and many of the local girls became trained in the technique. The initials J.S. crop up not infrequently on the hinge side of these brooches and J.S. is listed in the Sheffield directories of the nineteenth century from 1871 as a 'buffalo horn scale cutter and presser and manufacturer of horn brooches and ornaments' who worked from premises at 108 Arundel Lane. The initials stand for John Stevens who employed about thirty girls for this specialist work, and the finer examples are very beautiful indeed. Obviously the ones bearing the initials J.S. are more coveted, but it is worth noting that some of his work was undertaken for bracelets made up of

(Left) *Horn brooch with fine quality piqué work. Initials on hollow back J.S. (John Stevens). Last quarter nineteenth century.* (Right) *Buffalo horn brooch depicting hand holding floral wreath. Second half nineteenth century.*

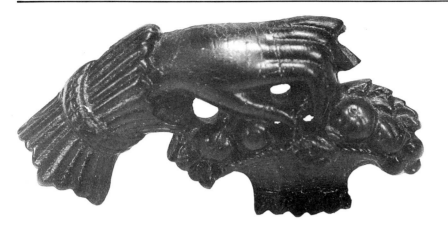

numerous brooch-like sections, joined with an expandable material like elastic. These sections were not hollow-backed and originally had metal bands through which the elastic could be threaded. Many of these bracelets have now been divided and made into brooches but the collector should realize what their original use was and that the hinge work will not be so finely executed. Regimental badges may also have a base ground of horn and there are many from which the collector may choose.

Numerous jet brooches were also made during the nineteenth century and it was not long before horners were using buffalo horn, of similar weight, to imitate the jet designs. Mourning jewellery was in fashion, particularly following the death of Prince Albert in December 1861, and so buffalo horn provided a lucrative and attractive answer to many horn-workers. Quantities of black brooches, clasps, ear-rings and crosses were made by a Sheffield man called Henry Townsend and the Grove family at Halesowen were quick to have a few dies cut and produce some really good examples. The horners simulated jet extremely well but if held up to a very strong light the tell-tale variation in the depth of dye will show. Jet, of course, is dense. A check should also be made for the very slight lifting of the surface which may occur on the back of horn brooches. This may only be noticed when close examination is made with a strong magnifying glass. It is particularly evident on the classic hand designs of the gauntlet and basket of fruit often wrongly described as jet or bog oak, although some were fashioned from these materials.

The Art Nouveau period is well remembered in translucent horn for there are a number of flamboyant designs incorporating butterflies, birds, dragonflies, bees and flowers . . . to mention but a few.

(Left) *Buffalo horn brooch depicting hand holding basket of fruit. Second half nineteenth century. (Maximum length: 5.5 cm.)* (Right) *Regimental badge, 1911.*

Horn books

(Left) *Seventeenth-century horn book found at Brasenose College, Oxford.* (Right) *Back of the horn book depicting Charles II on horseback.*

> When little children first are brought to schoole
> A horne book is a necessarie toole.
>
> *Breton*

The name horn book was originally applied to an elementary one-page textbook covered with a sheet of horn and called a primer, that was used by children. The frame of the earlier examples was usually a wooden rectangle with a narrow hand-grip, bound at the edges on one side by metal which held a transparent piece of horn in place. Slipped between the horn and back (similar to the principle of a picture mount) was the primer sheet. In the very early horn books this would have been hand-written on vellum or parchment, though none of these sheets appears to have survived. It would probably be reasonable to assume that the sixteenth-century horn book from Southwark at the Museum of London had such an insertion. The frame is oak with a thin strip of latten holding the now opaque, cracked horn in place with hand-tooled iron nails.

The horn books were not generally in use until the end of the sixteenth century, but earlier ones were probably made about 1450 and these would have been in black letters, but roman was probably used as well from its introduction in 1467. Black and

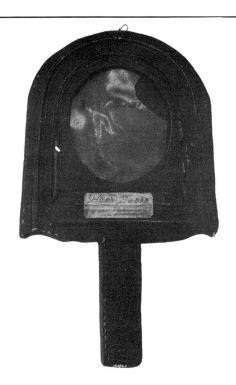

(Left) *Sixteenth-century horn book from Southwark. (20.7 cm overall length, horn area: 13×9 cm.)* (Right) *Red leather horn book in the shape of a battledore with a date of 1659.*

roman ran concurrently until the more legible roman type superseded its predecessor.

Dating horn books can be difficult, although some indication may be given by the shape, the way it is mounted and the type of printing used, although none of these can be taken as totally indicative as both repair and replacement work may have been done.

The backs of horn books were decorated in various ways, some, including the handle, with silver filligree – like the one reputed to have been given to Lord Egerton by Elizabeth I as illustrated by Peter Stone (*see* Bibliography). Others had decoration of birds, trees, and St George and the dragon, while many show a device of Charles I or Charles II.

It must be remembered that the decorative blocks could be handed from one generation to the next until worn out. To quote A. W. Tuer:

> 'It is therefore quite probable that a horn book which came into existence during the reign, say, of George I may have been reprinted from type set up in Charles II's time and backed with a block representing Charles I.'

At the Bodleian Library, Oxford there is a lovely example of an early seventeenth-century horn book which was found in the process of clearing ground for the new building of Brasenose College in the summer of 1881 and was presented to the Bodleian on April 20, 1882 by the Principal and Fellows of the College.

The book frame is of oak on which the printed sheet in black lettering is mounted and covered by transparent horn, which is held in place by a thin latten, some of which is missing. The latten is held in place by hand-tooled iron nails. Some restoration work was done in 1882 when the upper section of the horn leaf was restored, and several of the iron nails were replaced by steel pins.

On the primer sheet is a cross before the alphabet which starts with an upper case A followed by a lower case alphabet which omits 'j', shows both forms of 'r' and 's' and an ampersand following 'z'. Then follow the five vowels after which the alphabet is shown in upper case, again omitting 'J' and also 'V'. Below this is set the syllabarium in two columns, underneath which comes the invocation 'In the name of the Father, & of the Son & of the Holy Ghost, Amen'. Finally, on the sheet is printed the Lord's Prayer.

The Bodleian has four examples of the original form of horn book, the earliest one having been described in some detail. Two that are catalogued as being from about 1700 are almost identical in size with only a variation in the shape of the handle grip. Each is made on a wooden frame, one being covered with red paper and stamped on the back with the device of Charles I, the other being covered with terracotta paper with the device of Charles II on the back. They have an identical sheet of paper even to the decorative scroll edging. The type is roman, it includes all the letters of the alphabet, and the order for the rest of the printing is the same as in the earlier example described. The sheet of paper on each is covered by transparent horn held in place by a thin strip of latten and secured with iron nails.

The fourth horn book at the Bodleian is cut from a similar sized, but thicker section of wood and appears to be older than the two previously described. The paper sheet is very similar, again with the decorative scroll edging, covered with horn and held in place by a strip of latten and secured by nails which have rusted.

York Museum has a very well preserved red leather horn book in the shape of a battledore with a date of 1659. It is hand-stitched with the horn still preserved, but there is no primer sheet.

There are numerous nineteenth-century reproductions and it is known that examples have been removed from Tuer's

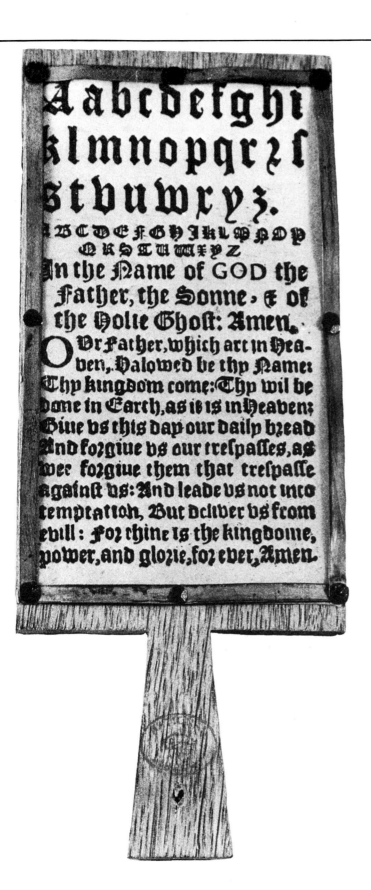

Reproduction horn books made for the History of the Horn Book, *written by Tuer and published 1896.*

Two views of a reproduction horn book from Tuer's work showing device of Charles II on back.

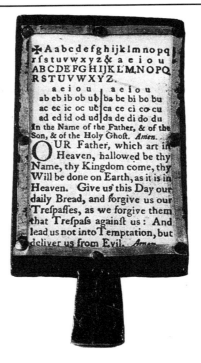

works and became collectors' pieces. When compared with early examples the mistake should be spotted easily. Regrettably there are many fakes in existence. The wood ones can be made using old oak, leather ones from old harnesses and metal ones reproduced from older moulds.

Horn books which do not have the protective covering of horn, although retaining the name, have not been described in this book. In the Bibliography (Appendix VI) there are references to works which will amply describe many alternatives and variations.

Snuff mulls

Snuff or the fan supply each pause of chat
With singing, laughing, ogling and all that.

Pope

The term mull has provoked much discussion as to the original meaning of the word and the explanations remain diverse. One of the more popular suggestions is that it comes from the word mill, reminding one that the original containers had a form of grater, or mill, to powder the snuff mixtures. Another suggestion is that when the word mill is pronounced in a broad Scottish dialect it tends to be heard as 'mull' rather than mill. This would seem an acceptable explanation since it is from Scotland that nearly all the snuff mulls originate.

The earlier examples of snuff mulls are generally known as bombé, Jacobite, or vase-shaped mulls because of their upright form, and they were made from horn as well as a variety of other materials. The base was inset, using the same principle as that described in the section on beakers and the lids were either totally separate or hinged. The horn may either form the major portion of the mull or be used as a decorative addition in the design of the lid. One example of this type has been seen where the container itself was made from lignum vitae, which is a very hard wood, and the silver metal hinge holding the horn lid in place was shaped like a thistle. The lid lining was of cork. It was a particularly interesting piece as the interior was cut vertically on one side at close intervals thus producing a serrated surface so that the owner could grind his own snuff. Vase-shaped snuff mulls were made from the end of the seventeenth century until the end of the eighteenth century when the design was altered.

Towards the end of the eighteenth century fashions changed and the well-known snuff mull made from the tip end of young oxhorns of various breeds became very popular. Their variety in shape, colour, size, adornment, and quality is infinite. The idea of inverting the tip as a container was not new to that age, but as a container for snuff it lent itself admirably to the hand of the horner. The actual tip was impractical to leave in its original form, because the point would make holes in the pocket of the carrier, so the horner whittled the tip to a narrower diameter, heated it and curled it into a scroll shape, some being more expertly dealt with than others. The result is fascinating. If looked at closely it will be found that the scroll in some cases has been fashioned from a flattened tip while others have kept the original cylindrical form throughout the scroll-work. Another point of interest is the ability of the horner to keep the circles of the scroll evenly distributed. This is not an easy task as one horner today who is experimenting with this technique has discovered. In nearly every example seen the lid has been attached with some form of hinge, varying from different types of metal to leather.

The lids are lined with a wide variety of materials to act as bungs. These include cork, ivory, leather, wood, horn, iron, and sometimes the extension of a metal washer coming from the lid itself. The hinges may be plain or shaped. A silver metal hinge seen in a private collection has been formed into the heads of two birds – a very charming addition. Sometimes the lid will carry a silver mount bearing an inscription or a mono-

Last quarter of seventeenth-century Jacobite-style mull with leather hinge and wood lining to lid. (Height: 7.6 cm.)

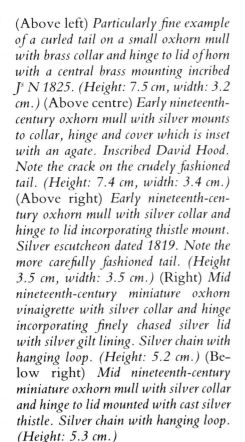

(Above left) *Particularly fine example of a curled tail on a small oxhorn mull with brass collar and hinge to lid of horn with a central brass mounting incribed J^s N 1825. (Height: 7.5 cm, width: 3.2 cm.)* (Above centre) *Early nineteenth-century oxhorn mull with silver mounts to collar, hinge and cover which is inset with an agate. Inscribed David Hood. Note the crack on the crudely fashioned tail. (Height: 7.4 cm, width: 3.4 cm.)* (Above right) *Early nineteenth-century oxhorn mull with silver collar and hinge to lid incorporating thistle mount. Silver escutcheon dated 1819. Note the more carefully fashioned tail. (Height 3.5 cm, width: 3.5 cm.)* (Right) *Mid nineteenth-century miniature oxhorn vinaigrette with silver collar and hinge incorporating finely chased silver lid with silver gilt lining. Silver chain with hanging loop. (Height: 5.2 cm.)* (Below right) *Mid nineteenth-century miniature oxhorn mull with silver collar and hinge to lid mounted with cast silver thistle. Silver chain with hanging loop. (Height: 5.3 cm.)*

gram. Occasionally there is a date, but without a maker's name or assay mark (which is very rare) this dating must be looked at critically. The lids are frequently adorned with a cairngorm, crystal, or agate mounted in metal. Sometimes these are mounted within a lid of horn while other examples have been seen which occupy the whole of the lid area apart from the metal frame to hold it in place and to attach it to the hinge.

The tonings and markings of some of these oxhorns are particularly fine and the horner having completed his work on the horn would have arranged to have various adornments added by the silversmith, perhaps, including a ring attachment on the wide neck of the horn, holding on individual chains anything up to five implements as follows:

1.	A pricker	– to loosen the snuff.
2.	A mallett	– to break up any lumps of snuff.
3.	A spoon	– to place the snuff on the back of the hand.
4.	A rake	– to smooth the snuff.
5.	A brush or a hare's foot	– to clear away any spare grains.

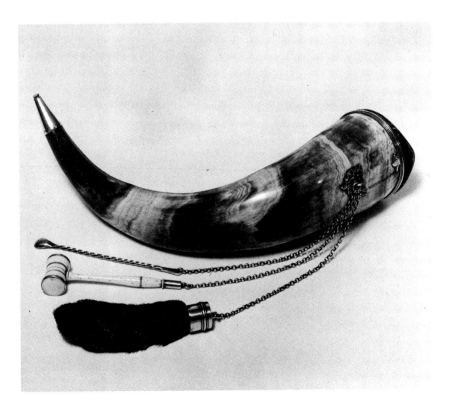

Finely marked oxhorn table mull with silver mounted finial at tip end and silver collar and hinge to silver thistle mounted horn lid. Three attachments on silver chains attached to ring on thistle mount below can. C. 1800. (Outer curve: 38 cm.)

91

The larger mulls were not curled at the tips for they would be kept within one's residence, and used on formal occasions at dinners when the mull would be passed round after the meal like the port.

Another type of snuff mull deserves very special mention. A horn tip in the hand of an artist could be worked and carved to the shape of an animal and some enchanting examples of this type of work have been found. The horner very often chose a horn with particular tonings to add character to the animal he had in mind. One of the most fascinating pieces formed in this way is that of the seal, for, as the colour photograph clearly shows, the cream beige toning of the body is perfect below the carefully shaped head with its well-proportioned ears and ivory inset eyes. It even has the wrinkled nose and the suggestion of whiskers. The patination of this animal is superb and is very much a collector's piece. (*See* page 122.)

Besides the animal snuff mulls one occasionally comes across a flattened mull not unlike a flattened powder horn, and prepared by the horner using the same techniques. Attempts have been made to give these mulls animal features. The tip end has been rounded, there are two eyelets made from silver, brass or steel and the pointed metal nose-tip snuff dispenser worked on the swivel principle rations the amount at any one turn! The earlier examples may or may not have a hinged base although the bung is usually made from cork. The later examples, probably made around the turn of this century, have a metal bar about a third of the way from the base on the inside, presumably acting as a truss to ensure the horn's shape. The earlier and finer examples do not have this feature and the patination of the horn is much finer. They are sometimes known as shepherd's purse mulls.

(Above and below) *Two views of a fine oxhorn mull shaped in the form of an elephant. The silver collar is inscribed 'Sergeant Edward Cooper 1821' with silver hinge to lid incorporating thistle mount surmounted with a masonic device. The elephant has a finely carved trunk with ivory inset eyes and ivory tusks.* (Right) *Flat sided snuff mull with silver mounts bearing the inscription 'To M. G. Robinson from Billy Moss', c. 1625.*

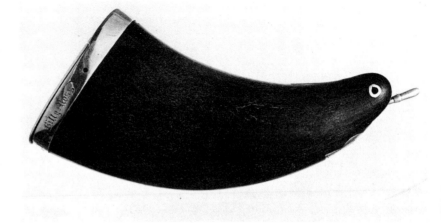

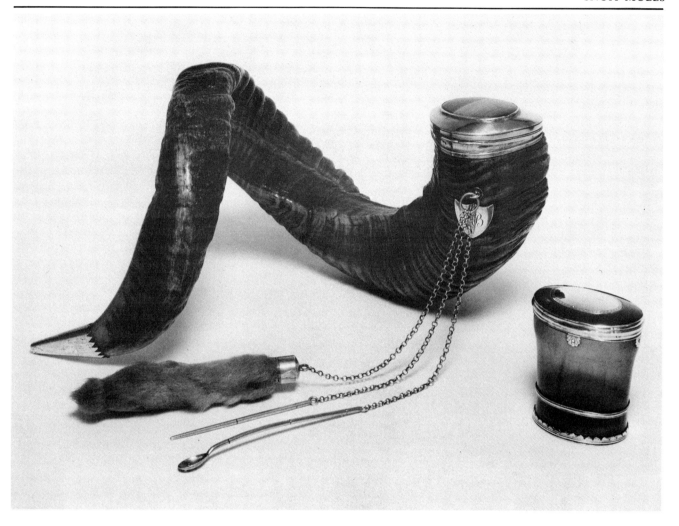

The use of the ram's horn which could be kept with its original shape was prepared and polished in the usual manner by the horner. The ridging and rich brown toning of ram's horn was ideal as it provided an ornament in its own right. The tip end was usually removed leaving a horn of approximately one and a half turns. The sawn end was mounted with a metal tip and the wide end capped with a metal lidded snuff container. To give the horn balance in an upright position a metal foot was sometimes added to the outside of the horn at the beginning of the first turn below the neck. The metal may be silver, gilt or pewter and the lid may or may not be adorned with an animal or bird such as an eagle, which was used as a means of opening the lid. If the lid is plain or set with an agate, it is usually fitted with a thumbpiece.

Fine eighteenth-century ceremonial ram's horn mull with silver gilt mounts to tip and wide end. The lid is set with an agate and the three attachments are held by a gilt chain. To the right is a translucent Jacobite-style mull with silver mounts, c. 1725.

Ram's head mull on three small castors with silver mounts inscribed above the hinge of the cairngorm-mounted lid: 'Presented to the Worshipful Company of Horners by James Holbert Wilson, Esq., Barrister at Law of the Inner Temple. November 2, 1846.' (Height: approx. 22 cm, width 40 cm.)

Ram's horn mulls were made for guild and regimental occasions as well as for use on the large private estates from the eighteenth century, and from time to time the taxidermist aided the horner as the entire ram's head was requested for conversion to a snuff mull. Some of these are rather bizarre in their form while others remain pleasing. The ornamentation is usually fairly elaborate. The tip of each horn may be found mounted with a gemstone and the snuff box itself is usually set into the central part of the forehead, the hinged lid mounted with perhaps a rock crystal. These ram's head snuff mulls were made with castors so that they could be moved easily from one person to the next at the table.

A number of factors must be considered if the purchase of one of these table mulls is being contemplated. Look at the condition of the horn in the first place. Sadly this has sometimes been subjected to a very brittle varnish, which cracks after a time giving the horn an uneven appearance of wear; others have been stained. It is important to remember to open the lid! A magnificent nineteenth-century example of a ram's horn snuff mull mounted in silver with an eagle rampant on the lid was seen on a stand in an antiques' fair in London. Unfortunately, opening the lid revealed a modern metal container holding a pottery inkwell. Someone had mutilated an otherwise prize specimen.

Taxidermists as much as horners vary in the extent of their expertise, and the general condition of a full ram's head snuff mull should be checked too. Clearly the type of mountings will be reflected in the price and the number of attachments which may or may not have been replaced. Many of these may have been broken or lost, but when present they do add to the interest of the article.

What of snuff itself? Professor Curtis has written extensively on the subject of snuff with a generous bibliography for those who wish to explore the beginnings and developments of this preparation in more detail. In general terms it has been documented that Cortez found that the natives of Mexico were using tobacco in a powdered form to be sniffed as a sternutatory or 'sneeshin' powder to clear colds and catarrh, rather as the Scots were doing in the sixteenth century for the same purpose, but using herbs rather than tobacco. It is known that the habit of taking snuff was introduced to Scotland from America in the sixteenth century. Many varieties of snuff from herbs were used for both medicinal and pleasurable purposes from very early times, but it was not until the seventeenth century that snuff taking became a more common part of daily life for rich and poor of both sexes. It reached immense popularity by the eighteenth and nineteenth centuries before the decline in its use.

At Bewdley in Worcestershire where there was a thriving horn industry in the nineteenth century, there are records which show that a Michael Holder and his son James made snuff. A dated trade notice of 1820 states 'James Holder's Scotch Snuff'. This was carried on in the old corn mill of the local manor. There are earlier references to the preparation in the seventeenth century in Scotland when Denune is recorded as having been a 'sneeshin maker'. No doubt there were many others, for a recognized and respected mixture may have been preferable to the doubtful results obtained from an individual's workings of a pestle and mortar with unknown ingredients.

> And from his pocket next he takes
> His shining horn tobacco box
> And, in a light and careless way
> As men who with their purpose play
> Upon the lid he knocks.
>
> *Wordsworth*

Horn boxes

C. H. Read wrote of horn in 1894:

> 'The brilliancy and evenness of the surface, the wide range of colours that can be produced, its almost plastic nature, and under ordinary conditions, its durability, point it out as an admirable vehicle for artistic expression.'

As a vehicle for such expression, the horn box was perhaps paramount.

95

Oval box with horn sides to base and top of wood with inset ivory panels dated 1688. (Length: 9.9 cm, width: 6.7 cm.)

Horn boxes vary in size, shape, colour, and condition. To be too confident in stating a specific use for a particular one would be foolish unless there is ample evidence that it contained, or was made for a specified concoction. Many of the boxes dated to the period when tobacco taking was popular are assumed to have been made for that purpose. In the same way the word snuff has been used indiscriminately for boxes which may well have had another function. It is well known that small and decorative portable containers have been used by both men and women in all walks of society for carrying on their person a variety of ingredients such as powder, pills, smelling salts, snuff and tobacco, to name but a few. Even if some of the boxes were made for a particular reason many have been handed from one generation to the next in a totally preserved and unused state because they have been kept purely for ornamental purposes, or even as a treasured possession to commemorate a particular event. 'Snuff box' has become a generic term for a wide variety of boxes available on the market.

Wood has been incorporated with horn on some of the earliest dated boxes, some of which are held by the Museum of London, others are in private collections and very occasionally one comes on to the market. These boxes were made in a variety of designs, including oval, round, triangular and heart-shape. The oval one illustrated has white oxhorn sides fitted to a wooden base and top. The two materials are held with minute wooden rivets with a bitumen type covering, and the work has been undertaken with immense care and precision, which may be seen if a magnifying glass is used. One or two of the rivets have worked loose and these may be seen quite easily at the top end of the lid. The wooden cover is inset with various shaped ivory panels on which the central lozenge has the date 1688 and a charming inscription 'To whom I lend it is a frend' has been finely graved on the four outside lozenges.

Another of these boxes, which all appear to have been executed by the same craftsman, or certainly by the same school, is one engraved 'The Sige of Namur 1697' and commemorates William III's recapture of the fortress of Namur which was lost to the French in 1692.

Samuel Lambelet who, according to Phillips, was a medallist to the court of Brunswick-Lüneburg, between the years of 1698 and 1727, was making pressed horn boxes during this period and, among others, the Worshipful Company of Horners has three examples of his work. These boxes are oval in shape with a separate top from the base – a design which recurs frequently in all attributed early boxes which have been examined in some detail and in some number. It has been suggested by writers on more than one occasion that Lambelet's designs closely coincide with one of his contemporaries. Phillips also states that he considers it was not possible that Samuel Lambelet either worked or lived in London during the period when the better known horner John Obrisset was producing so much work, which on the dated and signed pieces range from 1705 to 1728.

Phillips does make it absolutely clear that the many examples of the horn box with the equestrian portrait of Peter the Great of Russia were made by Samuel Lambelet to commemorate the foundation of the Russian Navy by Peter in 1714. These he identified from medallic portraits and corrected erroneous labels previously marking them. A signed box of this type is illustrated as No. 70 in Phillips's book *John Obrisset*. If very careful examination is made, the initials SL may be seen on the bottom left of centre just where the edge moulding begins. The Worshipful Company of Horners has an oval box with details which agree at almost every point, even to the border moulding. Unfortunately only the top half of the initial L is visible below the small flower, but its position and form must allow an attribution to Lambelet if compared with No. 70 in Phillips's book.

Here a brief comparison of workmanship has to be made between these two horners, because the Museum of London has an unsigned oval box of Peter the Great with a silver metal rim to the lid and a silver metal hinge holding the base. The

Oval translucent box of pressed horn depicting Peter the Great. 'L' mark attributed to Lambelet, c. 1714. (Lid 10×8 cm.)

Oval pressed horn box of Queen Anne signed S.L. First quarter eighteenth century. (Lid 10×8 cm.)

Oval box made by Obrisset illustrates his characteristic oval panelwork within the box, c. 1710.

base has an oval impression set in the horn which has apparently only been seen on examples of Obrisset's work. Also this box is identical in the details on the unsigned lid and border moulding to No. 69 in Phillips's book. There is a lack of fine detail by comparison with Lambelet's impressed work of Peter the Great. It would seem probable, therefore, that some of the boxes of this type were made by Lambelet and others by Obrisset.

The Worshipful Company of Horners also has an oval pressed horn box with the portrait of Queen Anne, signed S.L. and surrounded by the legend ANNA D.G. MAG. BRIT. FRA. ET HIB. REGINA. The impression is set slightly off centre and is a cruder execution of similar boxes attributed to Obrisset by Phillips and others, whether they have been found signed or not. Remembering that Lambelet was a medallist it is quite probable that some of these Queen Anne boxes should be attributed to the dies made by him as opposed to Obrisset. The dies were based on the medal struck by John Croker.

Further critical research deserves to be made between these two horners as their finished products have a measurable similarity and unsigned examples are nearly always attributed to Obrisset. Dealers and auctioneers who are only familiar with this name have fallen into the trap of attributing even recognized works of Lambelet to Obrisset. Most recently it cropped up in a London Antique Dealers' Fair where an oval box in green, pressed horn, depicting a group of men smoking, waited on by a maid, and a fourth man apparently attending to the needs of nature under a tree, was offered for sale. Even though the box was only in a fair condition, the scene was familiar and clear enough. It was definitely a Lambelet box, an extremely good identical example of which is in the possession of the Worshipful Company of Horners and signed by the maker.

It is also a point of interest that the horn boxes from these two makers vary in colouring from translucent oxhorn in some examples, to an almost dark laurel green, while others, particularly some of the signed Obrisset boxes, have an almost dense dark green toning. The shape is nearly always oval and it is rare to find a signed circular Obrisset box in horn.

Phillips has written very authoritatively about John Obrisset and for those who want to gain a more detailed knowledge of his background and entry into this country, reference should

Oval pressed horn box depicting a group of men smoking, attended by a maid. Signed S.L. First quarter eighteenth century. (Lid 10×8 cm.)

be made to the research which was published about him in 1931. John Obrisset came over from France with his family to England in *c.* 1686. His father was originally one of the Huguenot group of engravers in Dieppe and John, like his father, became an engraver, probably having been taught the techniques in the home workshop. No dated hornwork by him is known to exist prior to 1705 which is some two years after the death of his father, Jean Aubrisset, whose surname became Obrisset by 1691, as recorded in a parish baptismal register in London at that time.

Phillips states that there are records showing that Jean Aubrisset was a 'merchant ivory-worker' in Dieppe in 1676. He further quotes the term 'tourneur en yvoire' from the 1691 baptismal records in London, but he did not manage to find any definite records to suggest that Jean was active in hornwork in London, especially as his wife was left in very straitened circumstances when he died in 1703. Nevertheless, the possibility must not be overlooked that some of his work which is attributed to his son John, could be in circulation. A craftsman of some merit is not likely to put down the tools of his trade which would give his family at least some means of livelihood, and with no other areas of training having been recorded for his son John, the question remains unanswered, 'Who gave John Obrisset his craftsmanship training?' He is known to have been a maker of silver medallions, but there is no record of him at either Goldsmiths Hall or the Royal Mint. The Worshipful Company of Horners does not list him among their members for either work in horn or tortoiseshell, nor does the Worshipful Company of Turners. It must be proposed then that his expertise came from someone unconnected with these Companies. Why not from his father?

John Obrisset's boxes have a variety of his markings on them, which include OB in isolation. This initialling was used at a time when the first two letters of the surname by a silversmith were an accepted form of marking standard silver. This marking of OB occurs not only on the lid of a box, but also may be found on the inside of the lid, and sometimes the inside of the base as well on the same box, and the initials may also be set with a much bigger oval impression frame.

Other markings show a combination of OB with the rest of the surname in script with an '*l*' forming the first 's'. This is sometimes followed with 'Londini Fecit'. One writer suggests that I OB is another usual form of initialling, but the only example so far known is the one on tortoiseshell at the British Museum and this is mentioned in Phillips's book as being unique. It is followed by the first letter of *Fecit* just to the left of

Oval pressed horn box depicting the Judgement of Solomon. Unsigned but attributed to Obrisset, c. 1710. (Lid 11.5×9 cm.)

and slightly above the date 1708. Another unique marking is that shown on the Negro's head, one of only six round horn boxes illustrated by Phillips. The date 1720 is followed by the initials OB with Fecit set at the top of the capital B.

As far as records are able to show the final dating on an oval horn box with a sporting subject is 1728. This is a very rare example since the date De^{bre} 14 1728 occurs on the bottom left of the oval lid with the marking OBrisset. Jun. occurring on the bottom right just before the beginning of the moulding. Phillips again refers to this as 'extraordinary and unique' because he assumes that Jun. is referring to John as Junior in relation to his father, Jean, who, as we know, died in 1703. Could it be that there was now another member of the family with the same initials, since the downward stroke of the B has a decidedly different form and curve from any others seen?

Obrisset used a wide variety of subjects for the pressed horn work on his signed boxes which included portraits of Charles I, Charles II, James II, Mary II, Anne, George I and George II. Unsigned horn examples attributed to him include portraits of Charles II, William III with Mary II, Queen Anne, George II, Peter the Great and Oliver Cromwell.

The conversion of St Paul is depicted in both signed and unsigned examples and this situation occurs again in equestrian figures, Negroes' heads, and mythological, biblical, and classical subjects.

Probably among the most well-known horn boxes either signed or attributed to Obrisset are the Drake boxes, which are sometimes marked IOHN OBRISSET FECIT 1712. The date is not always included. One important fact which should be remembered is that Drake boxes were not always made by John Obrisset. Phillips mentions that Alfred Traprell, who discovered the initials I.P. on a Drake box either side of the helmet above the shield, attributed these initials to someone called Isaac Pratt, thought to be a worker at the same time as Obrisset. Phillips's illustration of this example is No. 101. The Worshipful Company of Horners also have a Drake box which has been attributed to Isaac Pratt because of the initials in the same position. This particular box has a very clear sharp impression from the die and the initials in the position as previously described appear to be I' I' when looked at with a strong magnifying glass. Is it possible that this die was made by John Jackson, a very fine woodworker turner in the middle of the eighteenth century whom Read mentions in his chapter in the book *Some Minor Arts*? With a poorer die impression the letters would not be so clearly defined, which could explain the suggestion of an initial P.

Oval pressed horn box depicting the Arms of Sir Francis Drake. The motto 'SIC MAGNA PARUIS' signed I'I' either side of the helmet surmounting the arms. Note four figures and thumb holding rope. Obrisset dies show three fingers and thumb. (Lid 10.5×8 cm.)

The mouldings on all the early horn workers' boxes, both signed and attributed, which have been examined, show a single, double or triple moulding beyond the pictorial impression. The boxes were made in two sections and generally remained unhinged. Another interesting feature of these early boxes is the slight bevelling of the horn on the inside top edge of the base of the box. Only two boxes in horn have been seen with a lid attached to the base by a metal hinge. One is in a private collection and the other example is that of Peter the Great at the Museum of London. All the hinged examples in Phillips's book are listed by him as being made from tortoiseshell or other materials. It is somewhat disquieting sometimes to find reeded borders which are sharp and show very little sign of wear in comparison with the die itself. Phillips's illustrations (Nos. 83, 87, 88, 91) show this feature. When seen close at hand on two separate occasions, one, where only the lid had been treated in this way, and the other where the sides of the base had been subjected to it as well, one has the feeling that this was a later decorative addition to an otherwise early box. The Victorians, as we know, added their carvings and adornments to much earlier pieces of furniture. Has this been

Oval pressed horn box (c. 1700) after the design by Hogarth portraying Ceres and Bacchus with the arms of the Lumber Troop. Motto 'In Nocte Lætamur'. Signed F.BAKER FECIT. (Lid 10.2×8 cm.)

the case with these boxes? It does not necessarily detract from them – if anything it makes the central impression more forceful to the eye – but the question here must be raised, 'Are they in an original state?'

Before going on to discuss later makers of horn boxes a reference must be made to F. Baker whose name appears on several oval horn boxes, two of which are in the Museum of London and another one which is in the collection of the Worshipful Company of Horners. In each example a pressed horn box with the arms of the Lumber Troop containing a lantern, above which is a pestle and mortar surmounted by a star on the right and a crescent moon on the left. Either side of the arms is a figure: on the left Bacchus, holds a chalice – on the right the figure represents Ceres and the harvest. Above the arms of the Lumber Troop is a barrel surmounted by an owl. The feet of the two figures are just above the motto IN NOCTE LAETAMUR with F. BAKER marked under the IN and FECIT marked below the LAE. A note attached to the examples at the Museum of London states 'This respectable smoking club (*see Old and New London*, pp. 114 and 116) held its meetings at Dr Johnson's House in Bolt Court, Fleet Street and came into prominence during the reform riots of 1830'. A footnote by Phillips in his book mentions such a box with the:

> so-called arms of the 'Lumber Troop' (an early eighteenth convivial society), whom Read has described in his article as working in the early part of the nineteenth century(!).

It would appear from the notes at the Museum of London that Read was correct in his statement as well!

Various names which have been found on horn boxes in museums, private collections, and antique fairs include Bradwell, who is first listed in the Sheffield directory of 1821 as 'James Bradwell, die-sinker, engraver and caster of typographic ornaments of Bridgehouses, Sheffield'. His circular boxes have good detail, although the name Bradwell is sometimes very difficult to isolate. His unsigned boxes are frequently attributed to Wilson, another nineteenth-century Sheffield worker, but the design on the base of the boxes is often identical to signed examples and can therefore be safely attributed to the true die-sinker. Auction houses have even catalogued them as 'attributed to Obrisset'.

Read refers to Wilson as a 'certain J.W.'. *The Horners' Craft* suggests Wilson was a contemporary of Obrisset, who died in 1731, and dates Wilson's work to the early eighteenth century. In fact there are three Wilsons, all Sheffield workers, at the

The characteristic shape of Sheffield horn boxes made between 1815–1855.

(Above) *First quarter nineteenth-century box depicting Burns and signed Bradwell.* (Above right) *The separate base is pressed with a central lozenge depicting a rosette on a hatchet ground. (Diameter: 7.6 cm.)* (Below left) *Circular pressed horn box (c. 1821) depicting Robert Burns and signed WILSON Sc^t. (Diameter: 8.3 cm.)* (Below right) *Base of Robert Burns box made by WILSON.*

beginning of the nineteenth century, one of whom, I.W., is mentioned by Molly Pearce in her article on cut-throat razors, and is the die-sinker working from approximately 1815 to 1825. It is this scaling work to which Read refers in *Some Minor Arts*. The City Museum, Sheffield, has a number of circular horn boxes which are marked either Wilson, Wilson Sc, or W. Wilson J; sometimes with the additional mark of Sheffield as the photograph of Caroline illustrates in the section on the Westminster Box (Appendix II). Reference to the inventories in Sheffield City Museum shows that these boxes were made either by Jonathan Wilson, or William Wilson and his son who worked in Sheffield from 1825 until about 1856. W. Wilson is listed in the inventories from 1825 as a 'bone haft and scale cutter of 55 Carver Street'. His name occurs again in 1828 and 1833 and from that date until 1856 the address given is 55 Westber Green, with a beerhouse being added in 1837 to the premises, and in 1852, combmakers' and brushmakers' engine manufacturer was added as well.

Although the horn box in the collection of the Worshipful Company of Horners only bears the name Wilson, it is followed by the letters Sc^t. The die for this box was without doubt made by William Wilson of Sheffield as the following descriptions will show. The circular box of oxhorn depicts a portrait of Robert Burns (1759–1796) looking at a figure representing his muse, and lettered round the perimeter 'The poetic genius of my country found me at the plough and threw her inspiring mantle over me'. Below the name Robert Burns are the words VIDE BURNS DEDICATION. Just at the curve of the left shoulder may be seen WILSON Sc^t. On the reverse side of the box is an impression of a plough with books, a lyre, and a thistle, while the surrounding border is made up of flowering thistles entwined with one another, which has always previously been recorded as being a band of oak leaves. Since Burns lived until the very end of the eighteenth century it is not possible to suggest this is anything but a very good example of a first half of the nineteenth century horn box, added to which Sheffield City Museums have two identical examples of the die impression in horn, which have just been described for the base of the Burns' box. The museum accession numbers are J1945.20 and J1952.35. The second number is a complete box of dyed oxhorn with the lid depicting a most precisely detailed woodland hunting scene. Below the caption TALLY-HO is the name WILSON. On the lid of an identical box (accession number J1945.19) W. WILSON occurs below TALLY-HO. It is in fact the lid of J1945.20.

Another circular pressed box lid with a clear definition of

Old Sheffield plate circular box, base of engine-turned horn.

(Above) *Old Sheffield plate circular box base of engine-turned horn.*

(Below) *The inlaid silver lid of horn of this box depicting animals and birds set within scrollwork. (Diameter: 4.1 cm.)*

Cupid in a bed of roses is marked W. WILSON J. below the word CHILD and at the outer edge of the rose. The engine-turned base is beautifully worked, depicting a vine in the round with bunches of grapes at intervals. An identical box, signed in the same manner, was on the market at Chelsea Antique Dealers' Fair in 1979. The verse around the border of the lid reads:

Cupid once upon a bed
Of roses, laid his weary head.
Luckless urchin not to see
Within the leaves a slumbering bee.
The bee awak'd – with anger wild
The bee awak'd & stung the child.

It is not difficult to find many examples of engine-turned pressed horn bases on old Sheffield plate circular boxes, and these form a most interesting collection showing varied and often intricate workmanship. Here again the tendency is to label these as being tortoiseshell. The Sheffield-plated rim and inside of lid hold the oxhorn in position. Frequently the inlay work on the oxhorn lids depicts dragonflies, squirrels, rabbits, and birds set within scrollwork.

The Victoria and Albert Museum has a cut-throat razor (*see* illustration, p. 129 above) marked '–illam and Rodgers Cutlers, Exchange Bristol' on the blade, which has undergone reshaping at some time. Gillam is both a Bewdley and a Bristol name; Rodgers spelt in the same way could well be a connection of the well-known Sheffield family who started in 1735. Unfortunately, in spite of repeated efforts, no documents are available in Bristol to clarify the origin of the blade. The relevant point to make from the comparison of the inlay work on these razor scales and the Sheffield boxes which may still be collected today is that it appears to have been undertaken by one particular craftsman. Could it be the Rodgers' firm of cutters who are listed in the Sheffield directory of 1833 as Joseph Rodgers and Sons, Jewellers and Silversmiths? Further research is necessary either to establish or disprove this theory for the design crops up too often on Sheffield articles to be ignored.

One writer suggests that imitations of piqué snuff boxes were made from celluloid simulating tortoiseshell at the end of the nineteenth century and that is why the gilt work, which was glued, works loose and comes away. It must be carefully checked that this description does not refer to translucent oxhorn simulating tortoiseshell, which was used to make many similar boxes at that time. From earlier descriptions in the section on fans it will be remembered that horn also has to be treated with glue when piqué work is combined in the decoration and there is a very real tendency for this to work loose in time.

In the early inventories of the late horner W. P. Dobson of Milnthorpe, Kendal, there are details dated 1819 during the time the firm was based in Bradford which show that there were frequent orders for 'miniature leaves', to be delivered to Deeton Hall and Co, Birmingham, and in 1820 to Maullin & Co, Birmingham, specifically for snuff boxes. The following year there are entries for these leaves to be delivered to Muntz & Purden, Birmingham, and Daniel & Geo. Holy and Co, Sheffield. Many other firms including Rodgers & Sons of Sheffield were supplied with these leaves. From these inventories it would appear that the Dobson firm were originally the main hornpressers preparing the plates or leaves for other manufacturers to buy and make into boxes. This procedure is described in more detail in the chapter 'The Craft of the Horner'.

The Kentucky Rifle Association came across an original catalogue of 'fancy goods from Canton, China, 1832', in which were listed '50 dozen scoops for apothecaries' drawers; black shoe horns, yellow shoe horns and horn snuff boxes'. It is known that there are many examples of horn articles which have a distinct Cantonese influence in design and artistry. Some of these are in museums and are described on old accession notes as being made from tortoiseshell.

Shapes of boxes cannot safely be attributed to any particular period but the shallow rectangular horn box was popular in the

A horn box depicted in the shape of Napoleon's hat carrying his badge. The lid depicts Napoleon a Moscou *in pressed horn. C. 1812. There is a variety of impressions commemorating events during Napoleon's life to be found on these boxes. The complete cockade is rare.*

Fine example of French pressed horn box c. 1820. La Bonne Prise. (Length: 9.1 cm, width: 5.7 cm, depth: 1.3 cm.)

A selection of oval eighteenth- and nineteenth-century boxes probably coming from the Humpherson factory at Bewdley, Worcestershire, with gravings applied by individuals at a later date. This is a characteristic shape from the Humpherson factory and there is an example in a private collection which is mounted with a brass model of a deer, identical to the ones sometimes found on Humpherson sounding horns.

nineteenth century and many of them were made in France. These are very attractive and the basic design is similar in all instances. The plain shallow base of the early nineteenth-century examples show without doubt that it was made in a shaped mould. The lid is joined to the base with a Mauchline type hinge which prevents any snuff getting into the joints and causing them to seize up. The design was originally worked out by a cripple, James Sandy of Alyth (1780–1819) in Perthshire and the principle is that of alternately interlocking sections from the lid and the base through which a long brass pin or horn dowel could be fed to allow the lid to open and shut. The only known surviving commercial cutters for this purpose are now held at Birmingham City Museum in the Pinto collection of treen. One writer suggests 'they appear to be modified watchmaking tools'.

The lid has often been subjected to pressing and the general design, and detail, will give an indication as to whether it should be early nineteenth century or not.

Mid-nineteenth-century examples of rectangular boxes, which usually have a deeper base, show a wide variety of lid decoration. This may include the poor quality tortoiseshell,

Buffalo horn boxes illustrating various forms of inlay work. Mid nineteenth century.

Box made from horn scrapings, mixed, boiled and moulded. The lid depicts GEORGE FREDERIC HANDEL and the base WILLIAM SHAKES-PEARE. Signed BARRÉ 7. Mid nineteenth century. (Diameter: 7.3 cm.)

Oval horn boxes in both natural and translucent oxhorn with either silver escutcheons or silver mount with inset gemstones, 1898–1937.

which is opaque; inlay work in various metals, bone, ivory, and mother-of-pearl; and rock crystal or gemstones set in the horn work. Some of the work has been painstakingly done and using the materials already mentioned the horner created a wide, choice selection for the collector.

There are boxes made from horn scrapings as described in the *Dictionarium Polygraphicum* of 1735 where the scrapings are mixed with calcin'd tartar and quick lime and boiled until the mixture forms a pulpy consistency. It is then dyed and cast in a metal mould. Only late nineteenth-century examples of this form have been seen and examined. It is suspected that the earlier examples have been broken because, with no fibres in the horn to give it strength, only the result of the recipe is binding it together, and a sharp knock will either crack or break a section because of its brittle nature. Two examples are in the collection of the Worshipful Company of Horners. One is a round box with a portrait of George Frederic Handel (1685–1759) on the shallow lid with an interlocking shape on the underneath to fit to the base. The outside of the base depicts William Shakespeare and just beneath the bust is the mark BARRÉ 7. This box has been engined-turned as the workmanship shows, not only on the lid and base, but also on the sides. This type of work is often seen on treen. The mark BARRÉ 7 could refer to a town in America where these boxes may have been manufactured in Vermont, but this has not been investigated.

The box lid has been crudely glued on one section of its outer edge where there has been a clean break and it is interesting to see that stress or drying cracks have appeared in the central sec-

tion of the base. It has a different feel from the unadulterated horn and is dense in nature. The texture looks different and the patina of age is totally missing. It has a semi-matt finish, and it is heavier.

The second box of the same material has also been engine-turned and is rectangular in shape, but it is not possible to examine the inside, as the top and base have been glued together because the metal hinge has been broken.

Towards the end of the nineteenth century and during the first part of the twentieth there were many examples of horn boxes in natural and translucent oxhorn which tended to be in two separate halves rather than being hinged. They are usually found in an oval or round form either with a silver metal addition on the lid or with a gemstone set in a metal mount.

Probably the most frequent gemstones used are brown, and rose quartz, amethyst, citrine which is a yellow quartz, and topaz. The smoky quartz is also known as cairngorm or Scots topaz, and the colour of this stone may vary from a smoky-yellow through to brown or even to black. It is extremely difficult for the collector to establish the authenticity of a stone as it may be faked. For instance, if citrine is gently heated it produces and maintains a topaz colouring.

Topazes are usually yellow or brown and may become pink when heated. An interesting feature of this mineral is that it will build up static electricity when rubbed.

Beware of one design which is currently being made in France and is a copy of a turn-of-the-century model. The new-ness of the horn, the shininess of the pins and hinge and total cleanliness of the interior should indicate it is like the modern example illustrated. Dealers may not be aware these are being manufactured and are selling them as antiques at an inflated price. Halesowen at Birmingham import them and sell them to the retail market. They are usually made today with a white oxhorn base, the lid of which may be made from dark-streaked natural oxhorn. The earlier ones which have been seen are of a more uniform overall toning with some signs of age.

Birmingham City Museum has a very lovely, early six-teenth century example of a pyx which was found in the ruins of Kenilworth Castle. It now has a hinge attached to join the two previously separate sections together when the pyx may later have been used for snuff.

A pyx was made for storing the consecrated host or bread and is an ecclesiastical term. The colour illustration shows an Italian pyx which was sold as a 'snuff box' but the shape, carv-ing and wear all indicate this was not its true origin. Only the convex centre of the base shows wear, because it has always

Modern horn box (1980) which is a copy of the late nineteenth century ones. Manufactured in France. (6.8×3.8 cm.)

rested on that surface. The upper half and its sides show an overall patination due presumably to natural grease being transferred from the hand to the cover when it was lifted to remove a consecrated host. It is made from white oxhorn in four sections. The centre of the lid fits into the ring diameter of the sides and the base has been formed in the same manner. It is a charming piece of carved horn as opposed to the pressed horn which is more frequently found. The name of the maker is on the box lid in Italian with the town from which he came and the date. In translation, it states:

STEFANO RUSCILELLI OF THE LAND OF SANTA STEFANO WHO MADE THIS BOX IN THE YEAR OF OUR LORD 1806.

The base of the box is carved in the round, in the same manner, the translation being:

HAIL MARY FULL OF GRACE THE LORD IS WITH YOU BEHOLD THE ANGEL OF THE LORD BE IT DONE UNTO ME ACCORDING TO THY WORD.

(Above) *Meerschaum pipe with finely turned horn stem in four screw sections and horn mouthpiece, c. 1867. Silver mounts. (Length: 47 cm.)*
(Right) *A pair of very rare eighteenth-century horn pipe tampers. Blackamoor: height 8.3 cm, Lady: height 7.8 cm.*

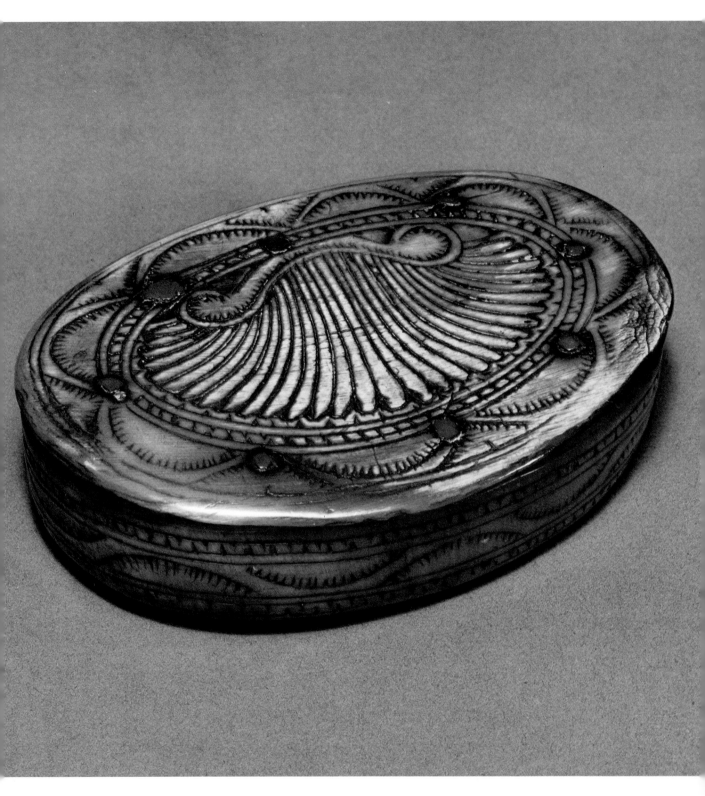

Fine quality carved white oxhorn box, probably Italian, c. 1580. (Length: 8.5 cm, width: 6.4 cm, depth: 1.9 cm.)

(Left) *A staghorn brush holder of gnarled and knotted form with the flattened rim flaring slightly from the main body, the patina a deep amber tone. Chinese 18th century. Height 11.2 cm.*

(Below left) *A rhinoceros horn cup finely pierced and carved including two dragons. Chinese c. 1700. (Length: 15.8 cm.)*
(Below right) *A seventeenth-century rhinoceros horn cup carved to represent a lotus flower with two small qilong to the sides and a three-legged toad to the rim. Chinese. (Length: 15.2 cm.)*

A rhinoceros horn cup carved in relief to include a boat underneath a pine tree, two eels on the deck. The reverse side with a fisherman in the water with an eel pot basket. Signed. Chinese. C. 1700. (Length: 13 cm.)

Triple-moulded late eighteenth-century dark oxhorn beaker. (Height: 9 cm, Top diameter: 5.8 cm.) (Right) Translucent oxhorn graved beaker, c. 1800. Notice weevil attack.

(Below) *Circular Italian white oxhorn pyx dated 1806 and signed RUSCI-LELLI. (Diameter: 7.6 cm.)*

Circular horn box with pressed circular panel enclosing portrait of Charles I in decorated armour. Surrounded by the legend CAROLVS: D.G.ANGLIÆ .SCOTTIÆ .HIBER- NIÆ REX. etc. Signed OB. First quarter eighteenth century. (Diameter lid 9.5 cm.) (Design based on medal of Charles I by John Roetiers in 1670.)

(Above) *German Gothic chest with iron strap work. Made up of 10 panels of oxhorn. (Length: 29.2 cm, width: 14.6 cm, height: 17.8 cm.) (Inside depth: 12.7 cm.)*

(Left) *Late nineteenth-century circular translucent oxhorn box with enamel piqué work. (Diameter: 4.3 cm.)*

(Opposite) *Close-up of the design on a nineteenth-century circular box of pressed buffalo horn signed W. WILSON J. (Diameter: 7.5 cm.) (See also p. 124.)*

(Left) *Silver mounted eighteenth-century white oxhorn beaker.*

(Below) *German powder horn with iron, brass and steel mounts, c. 1700. Because of badly flaking horn this has been treated with polyvinylacetate to prevent further deterioration. Notice lack of patination. (Outer curve: 45.8 cm.)*

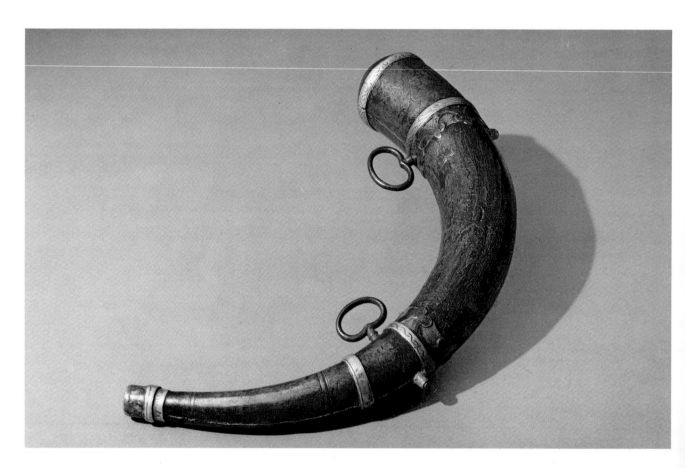

(Above) *Nineteenth-century ostrich feather fan with tortoiseshell guards and stained translucent oxhorn sticks to simulate tortoiseshell. Notice the merging and depth of colour in the guards as opposed to the sharp definition in the sticks.*

(Left) *Horn brisé fan exquisitely pierced and decorated with cut steel, c. 1810–1820. (Length: 15.5 cm.)*

Ox horn snuff mull with fine curl to tail, the wide end silver mounted with band engraved 'To Mr. Matthew Jon. from Mr. William Batty. July 1, 1821.' The silver hinge holds the heavily chased lid which surrounds the central mounting of rock crystal. (Height: 11.7 cm.)

Eighteenth-century oxhorn flour scoop fashioned from tip end of horn. (Length: 20.3 cm.) Fine quality oxhorn spoon with scrollwork along length of handle. The more translucent horn does not appear to alter its characteristics to become 'woody' with age, unlike the flour scoop. (Length: 11.7 cm.) Snuff mull of seal with ivory inset eyes and silver band and hinge to lid of horn, c. 1800. (Length: 8 cm.)

Late nineteenth-century and early twentieth-century examples of translucent oxhorn spoons and paper knives.

Examples of buffalo horn articles: rectangular box with tortoiseshell inlay; cross and tatting shuttle with mother of pearl and brass inlay; brooch with gold, silver and brass inlay; spoon of oriental design; Sheffield-style box. (See also p. 119.)

(Opposite) *Rectangular notebooks with case covers of buffalo horn inlaid with brass, silver metal and mother of pearl, c. 1860. Place Vendôme (9.4×6.4 cm); Fontainebleau (9.1×6 cm).*

A nineteenth-century beaker featuring a dolphin flanked by the royal initials VR. The opposite side is graved with a frigate. The design covers different historical periods. (Height: 7.1 cm.)

(Below) *Very rare ivory on horn plaques, probably Dieppe, c. 1785. (Approx. 7.1 cm diameter.)*

A selection of modern domestic utensils made at Abbey Horn Works.

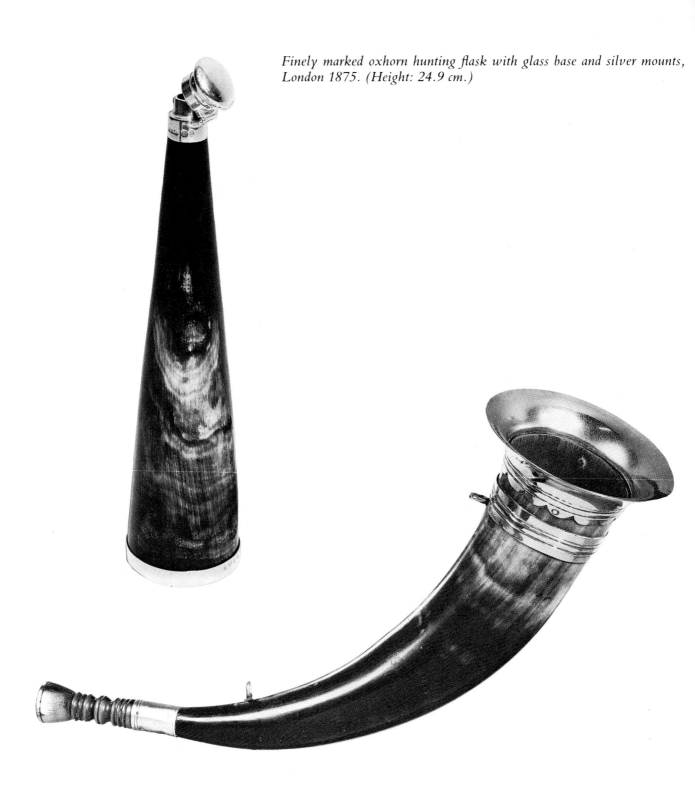

Finely marked oxhorn hunting flask with glass base and silver mounts, London 1875. (Height: 24.9 cm.)

Early nineteenth-century sounding horn made by Humpherson of Bewdley. (Length: 38.1 cm.)

The Sheffield grinder's a terrible blade . . .
A. L. Lloyd

Horn handles and scales

CUT-THROAT RAZORS

The end of the seventeenth century saw the establishment of the cut-throat razor industry in Sheffield but it is rare to find an example with a date prior to 1770. Many of the scale handles were made from translucent oxhorn, dyed oxhorn and numerous ones from buffalo horn. The decorative additions to these vary considerably from merely a brass or Sheffield-plate cap covering the rivet in the very early examples, to highly decorative impressed hornwork which was particularly manufactured and developed during the first fifty years of the nineteenth century. The dies used covered a variety of subjects. One of the most frequently marked scales comes from I.W., the initials of Jonathan Wilson, who was one of many scale cutters listed in the Sheffield directories.

The technique of scale cutting is described with great clarity in John Holland's book when he says that the

> moulds resemble a pair of forceps and contain polished steel dies, engraved according to desire. The horn which must be of the correct size to fill the engraved cavity of the mould, is inserted while the forceps are still hot. The pair is then brought into contact and immediately by means of an immense vice are so compressed that the heated horn is forced into every line of the dies. In most articles the horn is passed twice between the dies, the first time to mould the general form and the subsequent pressure to stamp the figure work, which is often very detailed and beautiful. On removal it is perfectly moulded and glossy.

The early flat-sided blades up to the end of the 1700s had no shoulder to protect the user from a thumb cut. These are easily distinguishable from the later examples and are a guide to dating a cut-throat razor. Very often the blade or tang had a maker's mark because of the number of skilled workers with the same name employed in this trade. Reference to the Sheffield directories of 1774 and 1787 will identify the mark with the maker.

At the very beginning of the nineteenth century, the design of the razor changed, with the introduction of the protective shoulder and the hollow ground blade which responded to a finer edge sharpening. Many of these blades have a variety of gravings. Some have national events like the Great Exhibition of 1851 while another shows on the one side the tools used

(Above) *Cut-throat razor with horn scales and metal inlay work (see p. 106).*
(Below) *Buffalo horn scales impressed both sides of razor, one showing 'Commerce' and the other 'Peace and Union'. No maker's mark. Razor marked ACIER FONDU.*

in the workshop and on the other the name Henry Leake, presumably the owner. The blade is marked Styring and Hadfield, who were cutlers in Sheffield about 1825. The horn scales are most beautifully pressed, translucent yellow horn with tortoiseshell staining having been used. The hunting scenes are illustrated on both sides of the scales showing the sequence of a huntsman with his dog and gun 1) charging, 2) morning, 3) shooting, 4) bagging, 5) evening. The sequence of the hunter's day is perfect in detail. For example, the evening scene shows the huntsman with his bag and the dog's stance transmits its total exhaustion following a day of expended energy. Beneath the word 'morning' are the initials I.W. standing again for Jonathan Wilson.

It is occasionally possible to find individual horn scales, varying in colouring, depth of impression and preciseness of detail in antique markets and fairs in different parts of the country. As collectors' items they make a charming wall display when mounted and framed on a suitable backing to bring out the detail, some of which is very fine indeed.

First quarter nineteenth-century razor with impressed translucent horn scales of gun dog. Reverse side illustrates greyhound coursing a hare. Signed Wilson. (Length: 14.4 cm.)

FLEAMS

A fleam is a lancet used for bleeding animals. The treatment may require the opening of a vein to let the poisoned blood flow, or perhaps more realistically to pierce an abscess, or to

Nineteenth-century fleam with accessories and oxhorn scales. Blade marked BUTLER. (Closed length: 8.2 cm.)

Nineteenth-century fleam with oxhorn scales made by J. Rodgers & Sons. (Closed length: 8.2 cm.)

remove a foreign body from an infected area. The all-in-one tool made by Butler, a Sheffield worker in steel and horn in the nineteenth century, shows not only the fleam itself but two accessories which fit into recesses in the horn scales. One is a folding knife of steel which is metal pinned to translucent stained oxhorn. The other is a pair of tweezers made of steel with a finger nail ridge at the closed end to facilitate removal from the scale. The scales are made from natural ox horn, steel pinned and with a brass lined case throughout. Some fleams, like the penknives, may be marked along the brass back with the owners' name.

Fleams were made with a variety in the number of blades and attachments. Two more are shown, one made by J. Barrott of Sheffield which has dark oxhorn scales and is again brass lined. This is the example shown in the photograph with the name Wm Dickinson. The second is made by J. Rodgers and Sons, descendants of Joseph and Maurice Rodgers who were Sheffield workers from 1735.

Fleams were very handy medical tools for those connected with livestock if quick treatment was necessary to ease an acute condition.

For the collector who is interested in medical instruments or bladed instruments these fleams may be bought at a number of antique centres. Obviously the ones which carry a maker's name are a more desirable acquisition, but the price tag will no doubt reflect the benefit too!

Nineteenth-century fleam with oxhorn scales brass backed with owner's name. Blades marked J. BARROTT.

131

Eighteenth-century penknife designed for quill cutting. (Open length: 10.5 cm.)

PEN AND POCKET-KNIVES

The Sheffield Cutlers' Livery Company was mentioned as early as 1344 and charters were granted in 1416 and 1607. Other areas in the country where knives were made were Leicester, London, Norwich, and York, but Sheffield was an ideal centre for the development of the cutlery industry because of its geographical assets of fast flowing streams, mill-stone grit and ironstone necessary for processing steel.

The early makers of these knives are listed in the Sheffield directories of 1774 as being makers of penknives which were specifically made for quill cutting as many people preferred to shape their own writing implement.

An article on cork modelling was written for the 1980 Surrey Antiques Fair Handbook in which there was an illustration of three folding knives used in the nineteenth century by Sarah Ruding Stevens of Quinton, Northamptonshire, who was a 'remarkable sculptress of cork'. To quote Jane Toller further, 'Her only tools seem to have been three long pocket-knives with thin blades of razor sharpness.' It is interesting to note that the one in the central position is very likely to be a true penknife because of the proportions of the blade, and since the fineness of detail in cork sculpting was essential the alternative use of this blade is not altogether surprising. Later on the term became interchangeable with pocket-knives, but the fineness of the blade suggests the true origin.

The very early knives contained one blade which would open and close into the handle and this was known as a 'Jack' knife. At a later date a spring was used to fix the blade into either the open or the closed position. The spring work was a highly specialized technique as faulty workmanship resulted in poor positioning of the blade in either its open or closed state. The blades were made from very high quality steel, the processes involved being:

1. Forging to produce the desired shape.
2. Hardening and tempering – a process of heating and then cooling.
3. Grinding for sharpening and polishing.
4. Finishing.

Once this process was completed the maker would use a sub-contractor for fitting the scales. All the pocket-knives which have been examined are lined with metal, usually brass, to receive the blade when closed. This metal 'guard' would protect the edge of the horn from being caught by the spring close of the blade. If this occurred there would be a layer split because of the horn striation structure. If it was subsequently left in the damp, further splitting would result – ruining the hornpressers' work and the tool itself.

As one of the photographs shows, a pocket-knife was sometimes made with attachments. In this example the blade is made by the Rodgers family, who had a firm in Sycamore Street, Sheffield, at the end of the eighteenth century. The attachments in this example are a pair of steel tweezers and a steel pricker, both of which fit perfectly into separate metal shafts at the end of the compartment for the blade of the pocket-knife.

Many of the scales on these pocket-knives in horn were fixed with silver at the rivet points and again at the tip end and along the back edge. Some of these were decoratively engraved. The horn used in these early examples was oxhorn; either in its natural colouring or made translucent through the process of boiling and pressing, before being subjected to an aqueous solution of nitric acid which created a deep and permanent yellow stain, acting as an excellent base for the subsequent staining, sometimes to simulate tortoiseshell.

Later examples have deerhorn scales some of which are in their natural state while others have been subjected to a tan pit or dye process to vary the colour of the finished article.

Georgian silver blade with engraving work and horn scales. Identical example seen with hallmark and maker's name 1801 Joseph Taylor of Birmingham. (Closed length: 11.3 cm.)

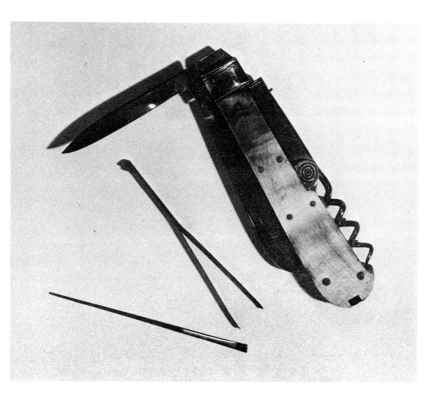

Nineteenth-century pocket knife with attachments made by Rodgers of Sheffield with oxhorn scales. (Closed length: 11 cm.)

133

Lock-knives were used as tools by people like sailors who often were obliged to work one-handed, but they could also be used as fighting-knives. When the blade is opened it locks into position and can only be closed by operating a special catch. Both Birmingham and Sheffield firms pressed oxhorn for the scales of these lock-knives into which brass motifs were inserted, a design particularly intended for export to Mexico in the nineteenth century. Many people believe these to be Spanish when in fact they were made in Britain.

Present day pocket-knife scales are still made from natural animal horn among many other alternatives, but it is the eighteenth- and nineteenth-century examples which will attract the collector for their charming horn scaling. Some of them have a mother-of-pearl and metal scroll inlay, representing the stem of the floral design, while others have included piqué work in brass as well as the pressed hornwork similar to cut-throat razors.

Nineteenth-century German lock-knife with steel blade and cupro-nickel mounts holding oxhorn scales with brass pins. (Length: 11.5 cm.)

CUTLERY

Examples of horn-handled cutlery have survived from the fifteenth and sixteenth centuries. It is not proposed to discuss the metal blades or tines other than to make one or two general comments as a guide to dating.

Until the seventeenth century most table-knives had pointed blades because they served a combined use as a cutter and a fork. Some later knives are found like this but the majority from 1750 onwards have a rounded end to the blade.

Forks had a variable number of tines but prior to the seventeenth century two was usual and these were generally straight.

The discovery of stainless steel in 1914 saved hours of labour for the cutlery cleaner who previously had removed vinegar and fruit stains by rubbing the steels with raw potato and then polished them on the knifeboard.

The blades or forks may have the makers' distinguishing marks, while any silver mounts like the bolster, which is the projecting shoulder of a knife or fork adjoining the blade to the handle, will probably have the relevant assay mark. Sometimes these are also found on the caps.

Early examples have been seen which make use of buffalo horn and dyed oxhorn. One particular eighteenth-century knife and fork set, owned by the Worshipful Company of Cutlers of London, illustrates the versatility of horn dyeing very clearly. The scales either side of the metal tang are a fresh, apple-green hue with silver mounts of shells and figured Saxon

English, second quarter sixteenth-century, single-edged blade knife with mark: a bunch of grapes. Horn handle of flattened octagonal section carved in Roman capitals with inscriptions separated by rosettes and fleur-de-lys. Obverse: BETER IT IS A POORE HOVSE TO HOLD THEN
Reverse: TO LY IN PRIS ON IN FETER S OF GOVLD.
Flat leather case with push on lid, decorated with tooled lines and stamped rosettes and leaves.
(Knife length: 19.9 cm. Closed case length: 21 cm.)

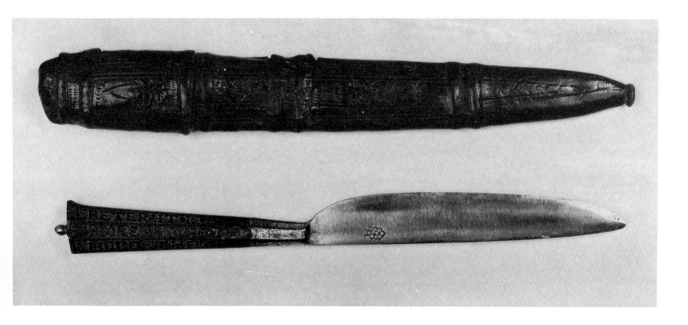

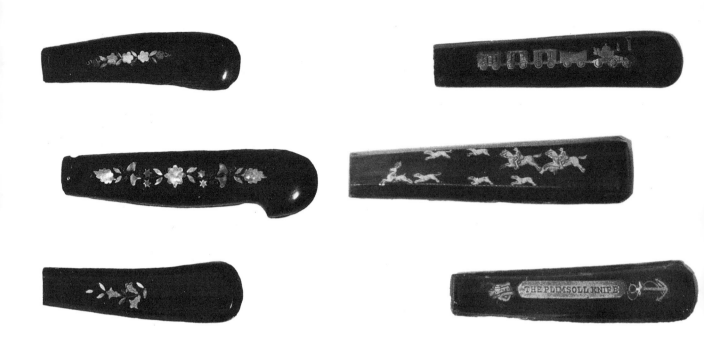

Three examples (above) *of third quarter of nineteenth-century buffalo horn scales with mother of pearl and silver piqué work undertaken in Sheffield, and similar to work seen on tatting shuttles.*
(Top right) *Nineteenth-century buffalo horn scale with brass metal inlay of train.*
(Centre right) *Nineteenth-century buffalo horn scale showing staghunt in silver metal.*
(Below right) *Nineteenth-century buffalo horn scale showing silver metal work inscribed 'The Plimsoll Knife'.*

miners. The end of the handle is mounted with silver lobed caps.

Buffalo horn scales were used extensively by the horn-pressers of the eighteenth and nineteenth century and these offer an abundant variety of design and patterning. Sometimes silver wire and mother of pearl inlay was incorporated, occasionally with the addition of both pewter and brass. To appreciate the detail in which some of this workmanship was executed it is well worth using a magnifying glass.

The pressed scales and handles were not always made by the cutler himself, although he would cut his own dies. This is discussed in more detail under the sections on 'Combs and Backcombs' and 'Horn Handles and Scales'.

Staghorn and deer horn have frequently been used for the handles of knives and forks for both carving meat and eating purposes. The staghorn, because of its natural ridging, makes an excellent grip. It is also fairly rapidly prepared by cutting a suitable section from its length, and cleaning and polishing before drilling a hole into the central area to take the tang, and fixing it in position with one of the suitable cellulose adhesives, cements, or resin mixtures.

Today very many articles are made using deer and staghorn, but the buyer should be wary of the poorer quality horn which has an open flint-type pith that is brittle. Efficient hafting is almost impossible to achieve as water will eventually seep into the gaps, in spite of the modern adhesives.

Staghorn-handled carving sets are both practicable and collectable, but quality does vary. Hallmarked ones bearing the Sheffield mark are worthy of special interest, particularly if the collector is fortunate enough to find a matching pair of staghorn-hallmarked carver rests. The knife sharpener may have a darker-stained handle. This is merely because it has been less used and less frequently subjected to the vagaries of washing which will eventually bleach the tan dye.

Second quarter of the nineteenth-century moulded buffalo horn scales with dots and reeding along handles of a set of six steel pronged forks.

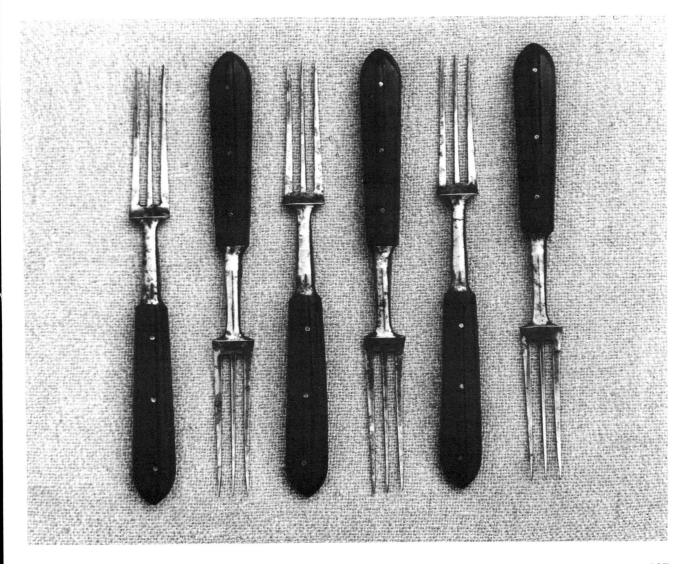

(Right) *Magnificent set of staghorn handled fish servers with silver mounts and engraved blade and tines. Sheffield 1882. (Slice length: 34 cm.)*
(Below) *Set of staghorn handled game carvers with silver mounts. Sheffield 1889. Harrison Bros. and Howson. (Knife length: 33.5 cm.)*

SPOONS

In addition to the handles for knives, horn is ideal for the making of spoons, forks and scoops. These were often made by travelling tinkers carrying their wares and equipment in chests like the one on display in the Museum of London.

Edinburgh Museum has an example of a spoon mould comprising of two shafts of wood held together at one end by leather thongs. One shaft has a concave bowl and the other a convex pattern to shape the heated horn to form the spoon. An iron metal band slips on to the two shafts which forces them to close tightly over the horn while it is malleable. The press remains closed until the horn is absolutely cold and set.

There are many examples of spoons varying in age and quality still to be found in antique shops and homes. The quality of pressing may be determined by the lack of evidence of any crease marks in the horn, particularly at the point where the bowl edge finishes and the handle starts. The handles may be of a uniform colour or show a marked degree of natural variation. Some of the spoons have been graved along the length of the handle, others may have a bowl decoration, while others have been mounted with silver work and mother of pearl or piqué. A matching set of six small silver mounted spoons may be seen on display at Inverness Museum.

Today, the process of spoon making has been speeded up by the use of electrical equipment. Spoons now are made from flat horn plates which are heated before being subjected to a hydraulic cutter to form the blanks after which they are heated and moulded again to produce the bowl. They remain in a

Spoons, Forks and Scoops

(Above) *West Wales oxhorn ladle with silver band at start of three-sectioned turned handle with whistle at tip end, c. 1800. (Length: 39 cm.)*

(Left) *Eighteenth-century wooden former for spoon with iron band for pressure closure. (Length: 35.5 cm.)*

139

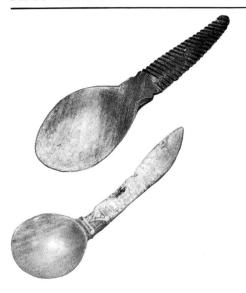

stacking vice until cold, before going through the three abrasive stages of final shaping and polishing which results in the beautiful modern examples seen in many retail shops. They remain a favourite non-staining, non-absorbent material for those of the community who enjoy boiled eggs! It is nevertheless surprising to find these modern spoons being sold in antique markets, presumably because comparatively few dealers are aware that horn is still being worked.

FORKS

Forks are made from horn plates, using the same principle as the spoons. The set of six illustrated ones was made in two sections. The tines or prongs with a short length of handle are cut and moulded from flat pieces of horn. In these examples the plates have been subjected to tremendous heat and pressure which has removed all the natural colour to provide a contrast for the dark stained handles.

Forks made with metal tines are described in the section under cutlery.

(Top) *Nineteenth-century combined butter scoop and scraper. (Length: 17 cm.)* (Above) *White oxhorn spoon of Scandinavian style dated 1885 in the engraving along the handle. (Length: 17 cm.)*
(Below) *A set of six oxhorn forks. (Length: 18 cm.)*

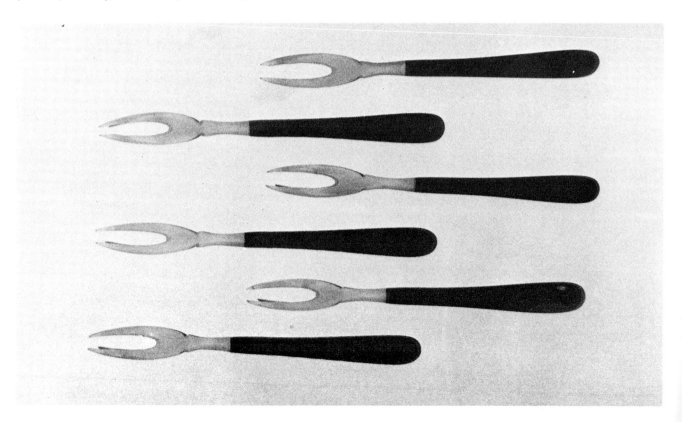

SCOOPS

Scoops which have a lovely rustic, time-worn feel about them may still be found in country areas and the variety of form, size and shape is surprising. They were frequently made from the tip end using that part as the handle while the scoop itself would be cut and shaped and fined down from the extending width of the horn. Very little if any heating was required for this design so it was a very cheap, hardwearing implement to make for farmers, shopkeepers and households alike.

Later examples became more refined and demand for them is still made today, particularly for the caddy spoon. The horners choose from a wide variety of horn colourings and the result is most pleasing and durable.

Eighteenth-century oxhorn scoop (length: 17 cm) and below early nineteenth-century scoop to show shell design on convex side of hand grip. (Length: 11 cm.)

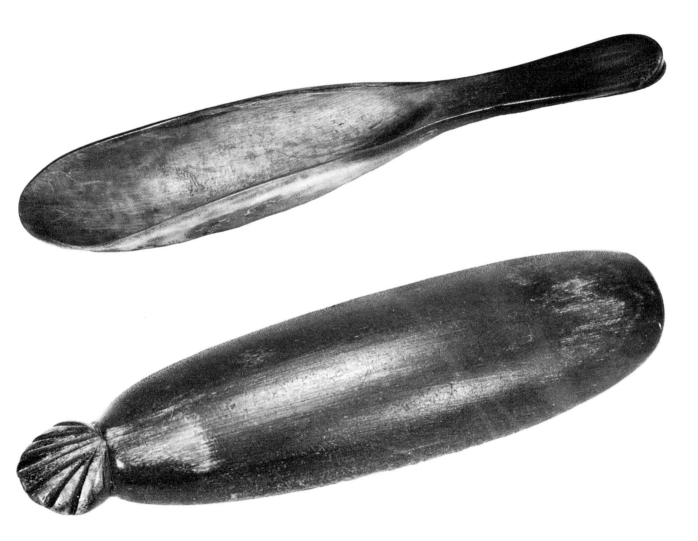

Spatulas and Paper knives

Antelope horn handle with oxhorn blade for use as a paperknife. Made at Milnthorpe c. 1920. (Length: 21.6 cm.)

A horn spatula, although more expensive than its counterpart in plastic, is more popular with the pharmaceutical industry because of its greater durability. Horn is non-absorbent, will not crack or split if well prepared by the horner so that no rough edges remain, and furthermore it will only smoulder if subjected to an open flame.

A spatula is made from any oxhorn from which the tip and the can end has been removed first. The better portion of the sheath is then cut along its natural curve before being heated and flattened into a plate in a hydraulic press. After cooling, the plate is again heated and once more subjected to very high pressure. This compacts the laminations, thus giving it strength. At the same time the tremendous heat and pressure removes the natural colour so that the horn takes on the characteristic translucent green hue. This thin plate is then fed into a hydraulic steel cutter from which the spatula is shaped. Following this it is put through the various stages of polishing before being ready for despatch from the factory.

The resulting piece of horn presents both flexibility and strength, an important factor for this particular product.

Paper knives are made in much the same sort of way, hydraulic pressure and heat varying in amount according to the type of finished product decided on by the horner. Some horn blades are fixed by their tang with a metal rivet into the dik-dik horn handle which has previously been prepared. The photograph shows a dik-dik handle with a neck attachment of wood through which a rivet has been fixed. These articles have been made from the latter part of the nineteenth century.

Occasionally one is fortunate enough to find an interesting use of a staghorn beam. In the example shown it is incorporated with a silver blade and hallmarked London 1801. The burr tip is also mounted in silver with the Crest of Lincoln College, Oxford.

Spatulas and paper knives are finding their way into antique shops where the collector needs to be careful not to pay inflated prices for the modern ones as these articles may still be purchased in retail horn shops. Again the mounting and state of the horn will give an indication of age. The quality of the translucency may be very beautiful indeed as the colour photograph on page 123 clearly illustrates, and the really good quality ones grace a desk whatever the period.

Staghorn handled page cutter with silver blade, London 1801, and the crest of Lincoln College, Oxford, at the tip of handle. (Length: 28 cm.)

Napkin rings

These very attractive items, which have been in general use from the beginning of the nineteenth century, are made from a wide variety of horns. The most easily adapted is staghorn, since it only requires to have the central section bored away and to be smoothed along its edges before being ready for use.

A section of oxhorn is probably the most versatile material for making into a ring and it is often found in translucent form, occasionally mounted with an initial in silver or with a plain silver shield. Sometimes the opposite side of the ring has an additional silver mounting holding a gemstone in place.

A silversmith, W.D. & Co, seems to be the most frequently recurring maker's mark found on both natural and translucent horn articles made towards the end of the nineteenth and first part of the twentieth centuries. Some of the more specialist pieces may be purchased with the original box and when this is so the Edinburgh hallmark of the thistle with the date mark usually accompanies the maker's mark. Not infrequently the silver mount is merely either W.D. & Co, or W.D. & Co .925. Thanks to direct help from the National Museum of Antiquities of Scotland who approached the Edinburgh Assay Master it has been established that the 'D' stands for the firm of Duningham who sent articles to Edinburgh to be assayed, from Aberdeen, from 1898.

It is possible to find the Cantonese influence in the nineteenth century on translucent napkin rings, which lend themselves admirably to decorative additions. As with many other

Set of three translucent oxhorn napkin rings, each set with a gemstone in a silver mount. On the opposite side is a silver shield marked WD & Co. (Duningham, Belmont Street, Aberdeen). C. 1900. (Average measurement diameter: 4.5 cm.)

articles of translucent horn they have often been stained in a variety of patterns and colours. A number of these may be acquired in tones from green through to tortoiseshell, and even to black. The effect can be very dramatic.

Today, rings may still be found where the natural and very charming colours and tones of the horn have been utilized.

These rings make ideal gifts, and it is interesting to make harlequin sets if the desire, the persistence, and the patience is there!

Get thee glass eyes;
And, like a scurvy politician, seem
To see the things thou dost not.

Shakespeare

There are very many types of magnifying glasses, which vary in strength and shape, fitted into horn rims which may be made from transparent oxhorn, simulated tortoiseshell, dyed oxhorn or natural oxhorn. The design helps to date them and here again an engraved date is a good guide but not necessarily totally indicative.

The principle for fitting the glass into the rim is similar to the process necessary for inserting a glass base to a beaker. A section of horn having been made ready by the usual technique of cutting, heating, polishing and making of a groove, is then heated sufficiently to take the glass. Contracting as it cools, the

Magnifying glasses

(Above) *Nineteenth-century oxhorn magnifying glass. (Closed length: 4.8 cm.)* (Left) *Nineteenth-century set of optical lenses framed in oxhorn with a brass pivot. (Closed length: 13.5 cm.)*

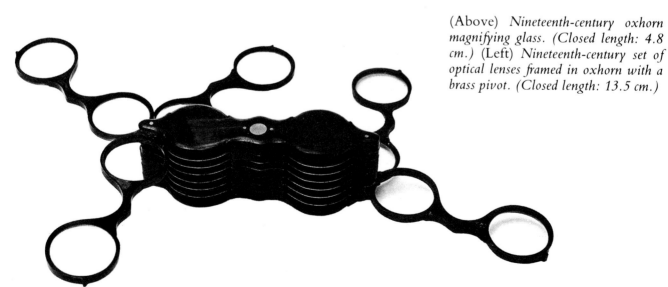

horn fixes the glass firmly at all points. If the glass is one of a set each one is mounted separately and after cooling the set is mounted on a pivoting pin, a suitable hole having been made in each horn to take the pin.

These magnifying glasses are still found in antique shops and the design, workmanship and strength of glass often puts modern ones to shame. There are some late eighteenth-century and early nineteenth-century designs which are very strong and totally safe for carrying. The size may vary from a very small one seen in a private collection, only as big as a fifty pence piece, to a much larger one which may be either round or oval in shape and has a diameter approximately of ten centimetres.

Stick dressing

And backward and forward he switched his long tail,
As a gentleman switches his cane.

Coleridge

A fascinating world of this very specialized craft was opened up to the author as the result of a visit to William Steele who was born in Dumfries and moved to Bowness for a number of years before settling more recently in Dorset. With unhurried precision he clearly explained the art of stick dressing.

The shanks, which are generally of hazel, are collected during the winter months of November, December and January, when the tree is dormant. These shanks are tied in bundles which are left to season for about twelve months.

In the same way, the varieties of horn coming from animals like the Jacob, Herdwick, Cheviot, Swaledale and other rams, the buffalo, the ox and the deer, should be left to season for about a year. This is necessary to let it dry out thoroughly when, as a result, there is less likelihood of trouble with the horn reverting to its original shape.

The equipment necessary for this individual horn work is very basic and a work bench belonging to a stick dresser looks much like that of a good carpenter. There will be a strong vice, rasps, files, a variety of drill attachments, a number of saws, chisels, and polishers.

Probably ram's horn is the most widely used type as it may be sawn more easily without splitting once the inner opening has been completely closed through prolonged and heavy pressure in a very strong vice. Added to which, this particular horn may be heated and shaped a number of times over a flame without it becoming brittle. Oxhorn does not have this

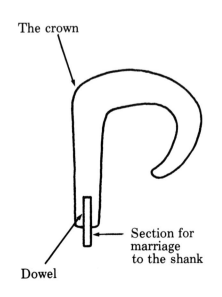

The crown

Section for marriage to the shank

Dowel

Bill Steele, a stick dresser, with a Swaledale ram's horn stick.

An example of a sagging head in stick dressing NOT undertaken by an expert in the craft.

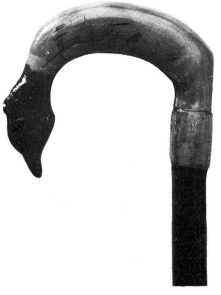

facility. It is important to have as large a horn as possible so that it is easier to cut, shape, and work.

The making, shaping, and whittling of the horn may take from a few hours up to a hundred hours, depending on the type of head being carved. The essential factors in the stick-dressing world are balance and size. Balance is brought about by correct shaping at the crown in order to avoid a sagging head, an example of which is illustrated. The size of the crook must be correct if it is not to injure the animal.

The marriage of the shank to the horn is achieved by various means including the use of a dowel which is glued into a hole

(Below) *Two and a half turns of Dorset ram's horn has been used for this magnificent adder stained to perfection and worked in one piece from the tip to the tail.*

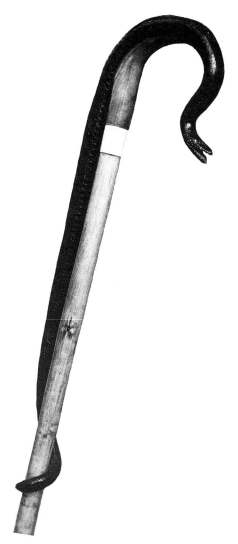

Sequence of photographs to show the gradual progression of work on a section of ram's horn.

drilled in the horn and is sometimes strengthened with a nail. William Steele prefers to use a bolt driven and glued into the horn which may subsequently be used for gripping the horn while carving and shaping it. This bolt is only used for ornamentals. Once the two surfaces are brought together they must be fine filed so that the two edges are of equal diameter.

Polishing is done with very fine wire wool, the use of scouring powder, beeswax, and turpentine, or a preparation like Brasso, and finally a rub over with a chamois leather. Some dressers use a hard varnish, but the effect is not nearly so pleasing, and in time may chip, whereas the true finish will allow the natural grease of the hand to continue its work of patination over the years. Varnish, however, is necessary to preserve the paintwork added at the final stages of ornamental stick dressing.

Many stick-dressers use staghorn which, if well-seasoned and of good quality, requires less work for the shaping. A thumb-stick is an attractive, popular, and very comfortable aid for a keen walker. The hafting is achieved by the methods described earlier, and the variety in the tonings of the polished horn may be very pleasing. It is easy to spot the high polish of a skull attachment to a piece of deer or staghorn as there is no ridging or colouring until it reaches the antler burr. This only occurs when the animal has been slaughtered or died before the natural fall of the horn has taken place. As mentioned in the section on deer horn, there should be no skull attachment beyond the burr.

(Left) *Perfect example of balance in this example of ramshorn scroll and thistle stick with stag horn collar.* (Right) *Derbyshire ram's horn showing sparring stag with fox. Staining has been perfectly undertaken with indian ink.*

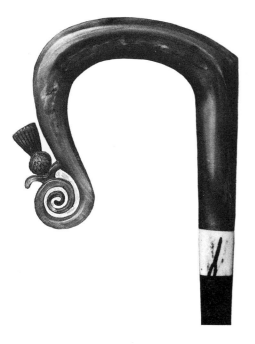

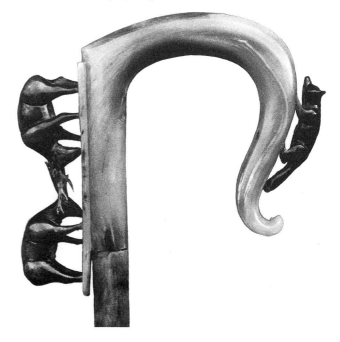

149

Nineteenth-century ram's horn umbrella handle. (Length: 14 cm.)

UMBRELLA AND WALKING-STICK HANDLES

There are many and varied designs of handles from umbrellas, parasols, and walking-sticks available on the market for the collector. Buffalo, ram, rhinoceros, oxhorn and staghorn have been used in a multitude of ways. Sometimes the natural colour of the horn has been kept, but with the added interest of a carved animal, with perhaps its features being inset with semi-precious jewels, mother-of-pearl, or ivory.

From nineteenth-century records at Sheffield it is also known that a large number of the umbrella manufacturers in Glasgow, London, and Manchester sent details of drawings of new styles required to the die-sinkers who specialized in the fancy dies including those for many of the animal heads which, as finished articles, were intended for the French and Indian markets.

CANES

Another form of horn-stick was made using a suitably shaped iron shaft on to which were threaded sections of different types and tonings of horn. Sometimes these cylindrical sections were allowed free movement and in other instances they have been found glued to hold each section to the next. Each tip was usually fixed with a horn or metal ferrule. The resulting stick may be most attractive and one dealer in Petticoat Lane in London suggested they were made for the use of the Edwardian dandy. The appeal need not be so limited, for these sticks are particularly strong and serviceable as well as being interesting to a collector.

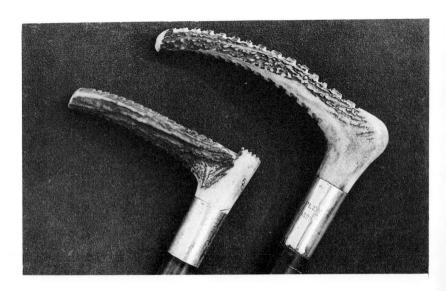

Staghorn crops with silver mounts.

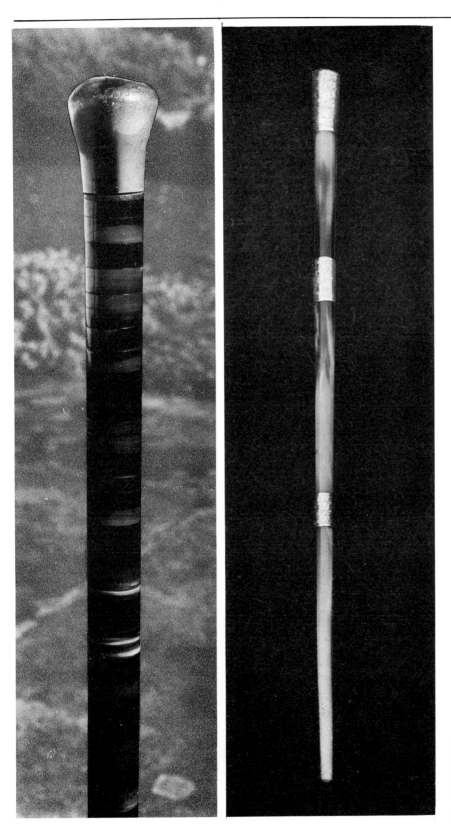

(Left) *Edwardian cane fashioned from rings of oxhorn. (Length: 80.4 cm.)* (Right) *Oxhorn conductor's baton with silver mounts. Birmingham 1895. (Length: 50.7 cm.)*

Chairs

Wondrous the gods, more wondrous are the men,
More wondrous, wondrous still, the cock and hen,
More wondrous still the table, stool and chair . . .

Blake

Many references are made to the use of horn in furnishings for there is a human desire to experiment with natural materials, to live with the result in some cases, to preserve the ingenuity of human skills in others and to immortalize the sport of hunting the horned animals. As early as Pliny, mention is made of the use of horns for decorating wood in his treatise on natural history.

It must be remembered that the word horn was often used to describe the exalted position of a warrior or king, presumably emanating from the fact that a horn was the chief weapon of an animal and showed a sign of strength, superiority and power and when related back to a human being, wealth often played a factor in its use. The fascinating story of the Waigal horn chair told by S. Jones corroborates the references to the use of the word horn for the purposes of the Chief or Head of a family. (For details of this story, see the Bibliography.)

Simon Jervis at the Victoria and Albert Museum describes the many articles dating from around the fourteenth century which may be found in European castles, houses and museums. It would appear that antlers from the stag and antelope are the most commonly used horns for the decorative additions to furniture of the nineteenth century in Europe, Germany manufacturing these articles in particular by such makers as Friedrich Bohler of Frankfurt who had a London agent in Cannon Street, and Rampendahl of Hamburg who exhibited at the Great Exhibition in 1851. Jervis mentions that the:

> large suite in the Horn Room at Osborne House is so close to the Rampendahl examples shown in 1851 that it must be attributed to the same firm and dated accordingly.

Bethnal Green Museum has a suite of furniture, attributed to Rampendahl, which is upholstered in green velvet. The couch legs are fashioned from staghorn antlers while the decorative arm-rests extend from staghorn tines to palmate antlers. These are in turn supported along the side of the upholstered back with both staghorn and palmate. Along the top edge of the upholstered back support, which is wooden framed, there is a variety of horn including ibex horn. This has been split and stained for balance of decoration. The central decoration has a circular wooden medallion mounted with the burr side of an

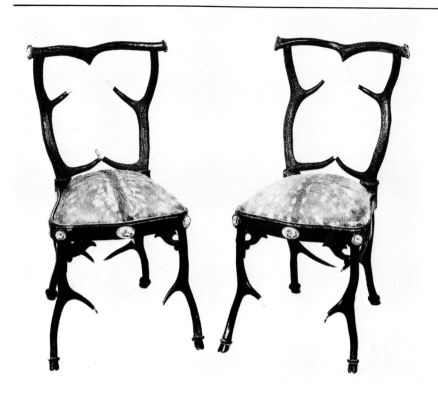

antler beam on which the vein holes can still be seen. The central area of this burr has been carved to illustrate both a stag and a doe. On the outside of the wooden medallion, a burr has been sectioned and mounted to form a decorative feature above which a single tine is mounted. At the end of each arm-rest the staghorn burr has been mounted with an additional burr, and glued to this is the carved head of a bloodhound.

The two chairs are similar in their structure to the couch except that the bloodhounds on each have been carved from the skull attachment to the burr which may be readily seen when examined closely. This, of course, means these burrs came from shot stags, or ones that died before the natural fall of their antlers took place.

The ibex horns are not split for the central mounting on the chairs, but the balanced flow of these designs is very carefully executed. The wooden framework of the upholstered back is decorated at the four corners with turned burrs, giving a slight impression of dominoes.

Palmate antlers have been used where one's body would tend to rest against the sides. The joining of horns to each other appears to have been carried out almost entirely with nails, glue having only been used for small decorative carving additions.

Oxhorn framed chairs from Texas made within first quarter of twentieth century.

Bethnal Green Museum also has a magnificent collection of dolls' houses. The contents of a room in one of these houses was given by the late Queen Mary. This room contains a selection of pierced bone and ivory miniature furniture which is particularly fascinating as much of it has been made to resemble a style of furniture made of antlers, two full-size examples of which are illustrated, and were sold by Christie's, South Kensington, in 1978. They are similar in many details to the furniture already described, which has been attributed to Rampendahl, and the auction house classified them as being of German origin.

America, on the other hand, made wide use of the Texas longhorns for the production of horn chairs towards the end of the nineteenth century. The Texas longhorn is descended from the longhorn cattle introduced during the conquest of Mexico by Cortez in the sixteenth century. De Villalobas introduced several calves on to the mainland and the stock from this Spanish source has continued since that time. Massive herds of these animals fed on the rich grass of the prairies and provided beef for the American market, while enlightened furniture-makers like W. Friedrich of San Antonio, Texas, made excellent use of the horns for the manufacture of chairs, selecting both size, shape, and toning with care. The pair of chairs made by Friedrich which are illustrated, were auctioned at Christie's in the summer of 1979. Each one is made up of ten pairs of beautifully matched longhorns, the translucency being a notable feature of this type of horn. The tips of the horns are mounted with acorn finials, some of which are missing. The glass balls – to move the chairs – are held in place with brass claws – a very typical feature of the Tiffany influence. The sprung, upholstered seats are covered in green velvet and have the additional superb workmanship of sections of well-matched horn veneer covering the wooden frame. The origin of these chairs is without question, as the maker's label is attached to the underneath of each: 'W. Friedrich Manufacturer of horn chairs and cabinet maker, 12 Crockett Street, San Antonio, Texas.'

As time went on, pure longhorns became scarce with cross-breeding taking place to meet the abundant beef consumption. It was only through the work of conservationists, who provided reserves to re-establish the stock in greater number, that we still have the Texas longhorns in existence.

7
STAINING, DYEING and POLISHING of HORN

Horn until now has frequently been looked upon as the poor relation of the tortoiseshell with the result that horn-workers have endeavoured to simulate the more expensive shell by working the horn in a variety of ways. They experimented with dyes, often with the direct intention of making the finished material difficult, in fact, sometimes almost impossible to tell from its expensive counterpart without resorting either to tests in the laboratory or the fairly well known and damaging method of applying a lighted match to the material in question – tortoiseshell will burn; horn will smoulder. In the laboratory, according to Herbert Smith, 'the physical characters of tortoiseshell show the characteristic mottling which is seen to contain numerous spherical particles'. Dr Spearman states that in tortoiseshell each horny plate has a new larger layer added each year, the old one remaining above it, thus making a number of growth rings, similar to tree rings, which optically would give a ripple effect. This is clearly demonstrated with the use of a microscope when the regular net-like formation may be easily seen. Dr Spearman also states that although both tortoiseshell and oxhorn contain keratin, in oxhorn the keratin is formed in cells which are arranged in fibres and when oxhorn is examined these fibres may be seen as parallel lines.

Antique tortoiseshell which has been subjected to light over a period of time develops a slightly dulled surface. If this surface is tipped very slowly at a variety of angles, the unique 'watermarking' may be seen without using a magnifying glass. The photograph illustrates this phenomenon quite clearly. Horn never shows this characteristic. Another point which is well worth remembering is the ease with which the layers of tortoiseshell may be separated, so that the maximum use may be made of this expensive material. The markings will therefore be clearly defined and there is a total absence of any striations within the material. Horn will be seen to have these, although it is more difficult to spot when the horn has been subjected to very heavy pressure and some of the fibrous content has been destroyed.

156

From the hawksbill turtle, which thrives in the tropical waters of both the Pacific and the Atlantic, come the most prized specimens of tortoiseshell. The specialist will look for the richness of the reddish brown pigment which has an almost three-dimensional quality and the mellow warmth of the translucent yellow ground. This type of plate may be worked to produce a very rich lustre, using a paste of cornflour and almond oil that is applied as a polish.

At the cheap end of the tortoiseshell market, shell is also sold which has an opaque appearance, leathery feel, and lack of any warmth of colour or polish. This type of shell may be found on numerous buffalo horn boxes of the nineteenth century in the form of an inlay and they make an interesting collection as the size, shape and depth of the boxes vary considerably. A uniform feature is the Mauchline-type hinge.

It may seem strange to discuss tortoiseshell in a book which purports to be on horn products from the bovidae group of animals but it is important to be able to recognize one from the other when many treated horn products are sold as tortoiseshell. Perhaps the most frequently wrongly described articles fall into the groups which include brooches, watch pair-cases, fan sticks, boxes, handles and scales, and magnifying glasses and spectacles.

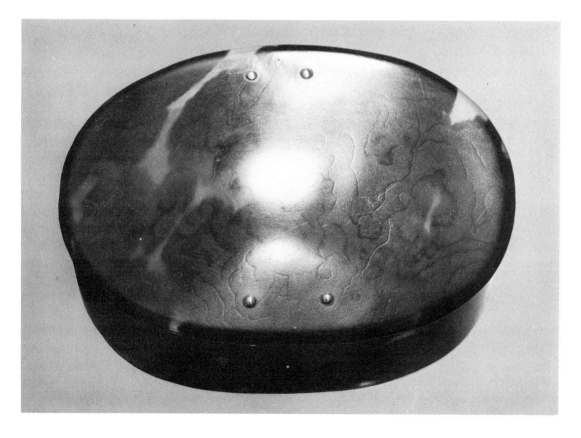

Nineteenth-century silver hinged tortoiseshell box which demonstrates clearly the 'watermarking' found only on tortoiseshell. (Max. width: 10 cm.)

There are a number of seventeenth-, eighteenth- and nineteenth-century references to the techniques used for dyeing horn to simulate tortoiseshell without details being divulged as to the precise quantity of any given substance. The oxhorn is the most generally used horn for this purpose. The tip of the horn is first removed and then it is cut along its natural curve. Following this it is heated in order to soften it, so that it may be prized open. The horn is then sanded to clean off the rough outer surface, before it is again heated and pressed flat in a heated hydraulic vice. The laminations are compacted which gives the horn extra strength, and it also develops a greenish hue as a result of the intense heat and removal of the sulphur. In days gone by, this enormous pressure was exerted by heated iron plates which had previously been coated with tallow to prevent the horn becoming too brittle. The opened horns were placed alternately with the iron plates rather like a multi-storey sandwich. Screw compression was then applied from one end. The firm Cornucopia uses a similar technique today with considerable success. Boiling and steam pressure methods will achieve the same result. This greenhorn, as it is known at this stage of processing in the trade, may now be subjected to a solution of nitric acid in boiling water. This turns the horn from its greenish hue to the yellow ground colour of tortoiseshell and the dye is permanent. The horn is then subjected to a mixture of alkaline compounds to neutralize the action of the acid which would otherwise destroy the horn. According to C. Tomlinson, the next stage is to simulate the reddish brown pigments by using a preparation of:

> pearlash [potassium carbonate], quicklime, litharge [red lead], and a little pounded dragon's blood, in a sufficient quantity of water. This preparation, after boiling half an hour, is applied hot to those parts of the horn which are to be coloured and is left some time on the surface. A deeper tinge in particular parts is obtained by repeating the application. A blacker brown is produced by omitting the dragon's blood.

The yellowish horn may be treated to many different dyes and there are fascinating descriptions in John Stalker's seventeenth-century book *Art of Japanning* with sections on 'the best black dye for ivory, horn, bone, etc.' and another section 'to stain a green colour on wood, ivory, horn, or bones'.

Rougier describes the use of the logwood chip solution which is made from chippings from the American logwood tree which yields a dye. The solution is made up of the chips boiled in water to which a nut-size piece of ammonia is added and the whole is allowed to boil gently, which results in a port-wine dye colouring. Certain mineral salts may be added which produce a variety of shades of amber, red, blue and green. Handles and scales, boxes and veneers of horn have probably been subjected to this dye which has resulted in the variety of colours which may be found today, many of which are extremely pleasing and attractive.

Black horn may be achieved by applying silver nitrate, which turns the horn jet black when it is exposed to the light. Many of the pieces of jewellery made during the very prolonged period of mourning following the death of Prince Albert were in fact made from black-dyed oxhorn or buffalo horn, simulating jet, as reference to the section on brooches will show.

(Above) *The surface lid of an oval box, forming part of a Cantonese late nineteenth-century dressing table set, in graved tortoiseshell underlined with horn and bordered with a moulding of oxhorn. The base of the box is stained translucent oxhorn simulating tortoiseshell and the sides are again in oxhorn.*

(Below) *This photograph shows a thin surface of tortoiseshell to which an under surface of translucent horn has been glued to give the article extra strength.*

Nineteenth-century translucent oxhorn backcomb stained to simulate tortoiseshell. Crude workmanship. (Length: 14 cm.)

Some of the staining work undertaken by horners is very artistically executed and the colourings and tonings are sympathetically used. Perhaps some of the finest examples are found on stick handles, watch-cases, and powder-horns. Natural dyes from fruits, shrubs, and trees are used. For example, raspberries will produce a brilliant red, while sumac berries offer a russet shade. A wide variety of greens are used for staining horn, some of them being vegetable dyes. Soot black from a kettle base was a ready-made source of supply for the artist and of course gave depth of colour to any engraving.

Indian ink offers a wide range of colours. For very detailed work, for which some of the highly skilled stick dressers are noted, it is an ideal colouring medium, but once applied to horn the colour is permanent, so the choice has to be made with considerable thought and care.

Much of the stained or dyed hornwork is very collectable and attractive, but in deciding on a purchase the buyer must be critical of the skill with which the work has been undertaken. Some of the examples simulating tortoiseshell have been crudely done, and the colouring is poor. There is sometimes evidence of a brush stroke being used for the application of the dye on the transparent horn; the staining has even been seen as a superficial varnish which has sometimes spoilt otherwise charming objects.

As mentioned in the section on 'Combs and Backcombs', a firm in Paris is manufacturing a variety of hairdressing articles which are on the market in some of the large London stores. It is difficult for dealers to keep abreast of all manufacturing trends, but it is fair to suggest that it is totally wrong to describe a piece of Halex-marked plastic simulating tortoiseshell as being the real thing. Ever since the middle of the nineteenth century, when parkesine – which is a celluloid composition – was first manufactured, purchasers of anything purporting to be of horn or tortoiseshell have had to look at it critically, as some man-made materials closely resemble the real thing. Artificial materials include bakelite, which was sometimes used in place of buffalo horn on the base and sides of rectangular boxes and for magnifying glass frames.

The field is wide open for further research into the horn articles held by many museums. Old accession notes describe some horn pieces as being made from tortoiseshell. Certain markings, mountings and stainings make this attribution unlikely and in some cases 'blond tortoiseshell' has the tell-tale mark of the oxhorn streak as seen on many of the natural polished oxhorn pieces. Tortoiseshell does not produce a marking in this manner.

In 1979, while visiting a well known and highly respected specialist shop in the West End of London, the author examined a pressed box of *La Ville de Rouen* which was attributed to Obrisset *c.* 1710 and marked on the ticket as tortoiseshell. It was in fact a beautiful example of translucent oxhorn, a similar example of which is held at the British Museum. The 'tortoiseshell' description was queried, the reasons were given and the label was changed. This fact is only mentioned to show that in a highly specialized market one needs to handle the two materials together in order to be able to tell them apart. The author has examined over three thousand pieces of horn and tortoiseshell and cannot stress too strongly the need to experience handling in order to develop the 'feel' of each type. It is not always easy when the workmanship may be superb. What it does strongly suggest is that perhaps horn is not such a poor relation of tortoiseshell after all, when it is not only described as such but bought and sold in all innocence at tortoiseshell prices!

8

RESTORATION and CARE of HORN

Providing that horn is not left for long periods in damp conditions it will come to no harm. Damp seems to promote the action of the weevil, which is a microscopic beetle that attacks dead horn. The weevil seems to eat through the surface area, but not necessarily penetrate the entire thickness. If the weevil is found to be active, it may be safely treated with Rentokil or a preparation of thiamole crystals before infilling the ravaged area if it is considered right to undertake restoration to this extent. It is possible to use a suitably mixed and stained plastic wood composition which, because of its structure, adheres extremely well.

Roughened edges and chipped tops of beakers, for example, may be smoothed with the various buffing tapes, but again the proportion of the article must not be lost. A certain degree of cleaning and polishing enhances an article which has collected dust and dirt over a long period of time, but over-zealous cleaning will ruin the antique patination and appearance. This particularly applies to some of the early rustic horn spoons and scoops which have only ever benefited from the grease of a human hand. To subject them to a spring clean, including sanding and buffing, to get rid of the lifting which may be apparent at the tip edge of the bowl would be sheer sacrilege. They were made as good, honest articles and should remain so. Their beauty lies in their natural state.

Horn which is becoming brittle or dry may be treated very sparingly with a preparation of Neatsfoot oil, and later a beeswax cream preparation which does not contain any silicone. The oil may also be used along both the outside and the inside of the horn hinges of boxes, which tend to become tight and difficult to work. If left untreated they may snap and then there is little which can be done to rectify the damage. Where lifting occurs on the edges of any article, or splits appear in the body of the article, the damage may again be stemmed by using one of these preparations.

Horn rejects many adhesives and as examination of St Hubert's horn in the Wallace Collection has shown, the horn was subjected to scratch cuts before glue was applied to hold the gesso work in position. Any restoration on these very early examples has to be undertaken with extreme care, especially when more than one type of material is involved. A German glue called Agomet is probably the best, but it is difficult to obtain other than in large quantities. A very good general glue is Araldite, of which there are two types. One is a rapid cure and the other a slow cure, the latter being the better adhesive for horn purposes.

Horn should never be subjected either to very hot liquids which will soften its form or to any dishwaters and their special soapy preparations. Household articles only require to be washed in warm, soapy water and this again preserves any glued articles from the danger of separating at their joints.

It is sometimes essential to prevent further deterioration to a piece of badly flaked or cracked horn and for this purpose professional restorers use polyvinylacetate. However, this is not altogether ideal for it leaves a hard shell on the surface, thus losing the velvety patination which is so prized.

For the general care of horn it is sufficient to rub over with a chamois leather occasionally, or merely to use the natural grease from the hand.

Brief History
of the Horners' Company

THE first recorded reference to the Horners' Company was in 1284 when John Pesemer was given the ordinances of the Company for correction. From this time the Horners' Company developed, although its powers were somewhat limited. For some time they only concentrated on the control of closing hours and the examining of those wishing to enter the trade.

In time more ordinances were added and by the middle of the fifteenth century a petition was presented by the horners to the Mayor, asking for curtailment of the trade, so that profits could be ensured and the horners' expertise kept within the bounds of London and those apprenticed to and practised in the art. The petition requested also that no horn should be cut within the bounds of the City because of the stench caused during the early stages of horn production. It has been suggested many times that as a result of this petition being granted most horners were found in the parishes to the east of Petticoat Lane.

In 1465, during the reign of Edward IV, an Act of Parliament ensured the right of inspection to be extended to all places within twenty-four miles of the City and to both the fairs of Ely and Stourbridge. It also appears from a document in the possession of the Horners' Company that during the fifteenth century an Act was passed forbidding any information on the development of uses of horn to be handed on to anyone outside England. However, demand for horn abroad was so great that the law was broken and the export trade flourished, helped not inconsiderably by members of the Guild. It was maintained that the export was only in 'refuse horns' and then only when the total needs of the Company were satisfied.

The horners in the last quarter of the fifteenth century joined forces with the leather bottle makers because independence was proving too expensive for these smaller companies. It must be remembered too that the use of glass was becoming more commonplace and this affected the continued success of these two companies. In the year 1476 a united Company was formed and the coat of arms, indicating three horns and three bottles, has continued ever since. This amalgamation bolstered the two trades for a number of years, but it proved to be only a temporary respite from the increasing use of glass. The bottle makers' side suffered more drastically, for their outlets were more limited and by 1567 only one such business was left in the City.

Discontent within the joint Company grew and discipline became more difficult to maintain. Orders from the wardens were disobeyed and those unskilled in the trade began to practise the art. Supplying and advancing loans to the king at various times; being responsible for the recruitment of soldiers; the storing of corn following a good harvest which would later be distributed to the poor; and the providing of money for the destitute, all drew on vital resources. Being released from these various commitments by Grant of the Lord Mayor and Aldermen, because of the poverty of the Company, certainly eased its burdens. With the death of the last surviving leather bottle maker in the City at the latter end of the 1560s their craft is now only remembered in the Company's title and coat of arms.

In 1638 a Royal Charter was granted to the Horners' Company by Charles I, and although the horners had to fight for survival on a number of future occasions, and

the supply of horns came from greater distances from both home and abroad, the rigid controls of the fifteenth century Act ceased to be so important. This was just as well since infringement of this Act had been taking place in varying degrees for a great number of years.

Prices were kept in control by co-operative buying. The export trade under the control of the horners continued well into the eighteenth century, one of the main products sent abroad being leaves for lanthorns. In 1663 as many as two million leaves went overseas for this purpose alone. As late as 1745 the Company upheld their exclusive right to press lanthorn leaves in the City.

In the reign of George III all control over the craft was lost, partly because of the development of the Sheffield horn industry, worked by the Rodgers family and others, and partly because of the growing public opinion against trading privileges.

As a result of these setbacks there was little to attract membership, especially without political rights in the City. In the late 1770s co-operative buying ceased and the apprenticeship list dwindled. So for the next hundred years the horners met as a member group of twenty or less to dine and to elect their officers.

In 1846 a petition was put before the Lord Mayor and Aldermen applying for a grant of a livery. Their request was granted, but various factions within the Company held back further progress. It was not until 1882 that the fortunes of the Guild changed when an exhibition was mounted by them at the Mansion House from October 18 to 20. Over seven thousand people came to the exhibition, which was a very large attendance for those days. Regrettably this did not bring about the increase in trade that had been hoped for, but membership rose steadily to two hundred between 1882 and 1925.

By 1929 the Horners had a large and distinguished membership, a charitable fund and full livery rights. They had achieved again a rightful place among the City companies.

From 1946 the Company encouraged members of the plastics industry to become liverymen in the Horners' Company, as many items previously made of horn were being replaced by plastic and some members had a vested interest in both fields. This ensured a continuation of the Company's contribution to City life. Although the Company retains its original title and coat of arms, it now sponsors a Horners' award for design and innovation in plastics. In its turn the plastics industry gives a considerable amount of financial support towards the cost of the Horners' float which depicts both horn and plastic products in the Lord Mayor's procession.

As the Horners' Company have no hall of their own, court meetings, luncheons and dinners are held in various City Livery Halls with the main function of the year, the livery banquet, being always held, as a privilege, at the Mansion House, by courtesy of the Lord Mayor. At this banquet the Brookeborough quaich is used solely by the Lord Mayor and the Master of the Company to pledge to each other prior to the passing round of the Loving Cup. This quaich, which is a fine spread of antlers with a small silver-gilt drinking bowl set in the base, was presented by Lord Brookeborough to the Company when he was Master in 1959. The Company have two silver mounted drinking horns known as the Hughes and Pinker Horns, donated in 1975 and used by the Upper and Renter Wardens at luncheons and dinners when the Master takes wine with his Wardens. The Master also has two ceremonial horns, one dating from the nineteenth century, the other being modern and presented by the firm of Cornucopia. Apart from these items and the Narwhal Horn which is inscribed 'The Horn of a Sea Unicorn taken in the Greenland Seas by the ship *Brittania* of London in the year 1801' and is carried at official functions of the Company in the Mansion House, the horners have now no other ceremonial plate of their own.

The fortunes of the Worshipful Company of Horners will no doubt continue to flourish because of its connections with the plastics industry, and because of the natural desire to preserve the ancient craft of hornware adapted for present-day needs in a market place where so much else is artificial.

Appendix II

Two Famous Horn Items

THE WESTMINSTER TOBACCO BOX

MANY fine examples of horn and hornwork are set in silver. Perhaps one of the most intriguing stories in this connection is the background and history of the Westminster box. It is, in fact, made up of a series of boxes, each one fitting into the other, which was started in its original form by Henry Monck. He was a barber surgeon, living at the time at Boreman's Court where the Treasury now stands in Whitehall. Henry Monck was an Overseer of the Poor, who was responsible for the needs of the poor and the destitute. The post of Overseer also included the management of the workhouse, the distribution of funds and the detection of imposters. A group of collectors and Overseers had been in existence since 1535, but it was not until 1724 that the Parish Council was formed. It is known that Monck, along with his fellow Overseers, met at regular monthly intervals in the Old Palace Yard, at least from 1713. It was here that Monck brought the 'kernel' of the tobacco box, a charming oval translucent oxhorn lidded box, the separate base of which was natural oxhorn. Tradition holds that this box was bought by him at the Charlton Fair for the sum of fourpence. It is similar in size and shape to the many oval pressed horn boxes attributed to Obrisset, Lambelet and Baker, but in its original form appears to have been totally undecorated. The horn box which measures $4\frac{1}{2}$ in. $\times 3\frac{3}{4}$ in. $\times 1\frac{1}{4}$ in. weighs $10\frac{1}{2}$ oz. holds about three ounces of tobacco.

The group of Overseers formed themselves into a society known as the Past Overseers' Society. It was made up of individuals who had either been elected as Overseers for one year in the parishes of St Margaret's or St John's, Westminster, or by those who had paid a fine to be excused from serving in that capacity. The Clerk to the Governors of the Poor, from his close connections with parochial matters, acted as secretary and was also a member. Occasionally honorary members were admitted for services to the Society, but such occurrences were rare. Monck, who had shared in the office and membership of the Society and attended

168

meetings to talk over parochial matters and smoke pipes 'in friendly intercourse', decided to present the Society with the tobacco box for the 'general use of its members'. Monck died in 1720 and as a mark of respect to the donor the Past Overseers replaced the horn rim of the box with a silver rim on which his name was engraved in the following manner. 'Given by Henry Monck, one of the Overseers of St Margaret's, Westminster, 1713 and repaired with this rim by Wm Winsor, Saml Board, Thomas Bird, Alexander Gibbert, Thos Newell and John Newell, Overs^s 1720. This was the beginning of the custom which has continued for some two hundred and seventy years. An overseer, being elected as custodian of the box, was able to add embellishments to the horn box or subsequent boxes annually, depicting either historical events, or events of some national importance, often accompanied by the names of the overseers responsible for the addition. Hence the box has become a fascinating, memorable, pictorial and graphic monument to Britain through the ages from 1713, with an increase in height of the original box from a little over one inch to the present-day imposing structure of forty inches (1 metre).

The several parts of the box, with the dates of each succeeding separate item, are made up as follows:

1.	The oval horn box	1713–1748
	(1799 small tobacco stopper and chain added to horn box)	
2.	The first oval case	1749–1782
3.	The second oval case	1783–1790
4.	The octagonal case	1791–1808
5.	The circular casket	1809–1826
6.	The rosewood octagonal cabinet	1827–1877
7.	The abbey oaken case	1878–1935
8.	First Tudor rose dish	1936–1953
9.	Second Tudor rose dish	1954–

One or two additions deserve particular mention, one being the portrait of the Duke of Cumberland, who in 1746 defeated the Scots at the Battle of Culloden. This addition was designed and illustrated by William Hogarth and engraved on the inside of the silver mounted lid of the original horn box. Silver mounted on the outside lid of the horn box is a portcullis – symbol of the City of Westminster. The engraving on the outer edge of the Westminster Arms states, 'This box to be delivered to every succeeding Sett of Overseers on penalty of 5 guineas.'

Another inscription on the fifth container, which is the circular casket, depicts Queen Caroline at her trial in 1820. This one presumably was added because of the preceding years of trauma at court which came to a head when George IV, as Regent, was pressurized into his marriage with Caroline of Brunswick by his father in order to get his debts settled. It was an unfortunate union as the Regent had already entered into another marriage (morganatic). The Prince of Wales separated himself from Caroline immediately after the birth of their only child. The princess allowed herself freedoms and indiscretions which ended with her banishment from

Natural variation of oxhorn depicted in this impressed box by Wilson of Sheffield, showing Queen Caroline's form of dress during her trial. (Diameter: 8.3 cm.)

court society and she retired to Italy in 1814, only to return to England in 1820 to claim her right to the title of queen when her husband succeeded to the throne. The king refused her right of title, ordered her name to be omitted from the Prayer Book and refused her any royal honours. The king started divorce proceedings in the House of Lords which is commemorated by the Past Overseers' Society with a picture of the trial at Westminster Hall and an inscription. It is said that she drove every day to Westminster Hall, 'dressed in a black wig with voluminous curls, an episcopal gown with a ruff, and a hat crowned by ostrich plumes'. The proceedings had to be abandoned because of the intense popular support that Caroline was given in spite of very strongly substantiated stories presented by witnesses as to her continual indiscretions in Italy with Bergani.

The story of her attire is pictorially supported by a Sheffield horner, Wilson, who made a number of pressed horn boxes from oxhorn. This particular one shows the queen very clearly and leaves the beholder in no doubt as to the designer of the die and his town of origin. (For further examples and dating of Wilson's work, *see* the section on 'Horn Boxes'.)

Other events commemorated on the box include the Battle of Trafalgar; the destruction in 1834 of both Houses of Parliament by fire; the Great Exhibition in 1851; and innumerable annual events of note up to the present day, which includes the introduction of decimal currency on February 15, 1971 with the inscription:

> Decimal currency introduced; the major unit being the pound, equal to one pound sterling and divided into one hundred new pence. This change caused the disappearance of the half crown.

On October 28 of the same year the inscription reads:

> The House of Commons carried by a majority of 112 votes a motion 'That this House approves the Government's decision of principle to join the European Communities on the basis of the arrangements which have been negotiated'.

By the London Government Act of 1899,

> the ancient office of Overseer within the Metropolis outside the City became, in effect, abrogated, and the new borough councils became the 'Overseers' for the purpose of carrying out certain duties which still devolved upon such. Thus quietly, and almost by a side wind, an ancient and historic office which had for over three hundred years played so important a part in the municipal and parochial administration, have passed away into the midst of things that have been.

The Overseers from this time became a Society who in the words of Dr Fisher in 1949 stated at the dinner

> 'This Club is a typical English institution – formed for a function it has ceased to perform; an anomaly which nothing can excuse except its existence.'

Those eligible for membership are Westminster men and women who have been ratepayers for a period of not less than five years on property in the united parishes of St Margaret's and St John's; directors or managers for the same period of companies occupying premises in the united parishes, the rector and church wardens, past and present, of St Margaret's and St John's; officers and servants of the Crown stationed for service in the united parishes; the persons representing Westminster in Parliament or on the London County Council and members of the Westminster City Council.

Combined with the Westminster tobacco box as part of the treasures of the Overseers' Society are:

The St John's snuff box made of horn, which originated with St John's Vestry Club in 1801 and was transferred to the Society in 1911; and the Trafalgar cigar box, originated by St Margaret's Vestry Club in 1806 to commemorate Nelson's victory and death and transferred to the Overseers' Society in 1906.

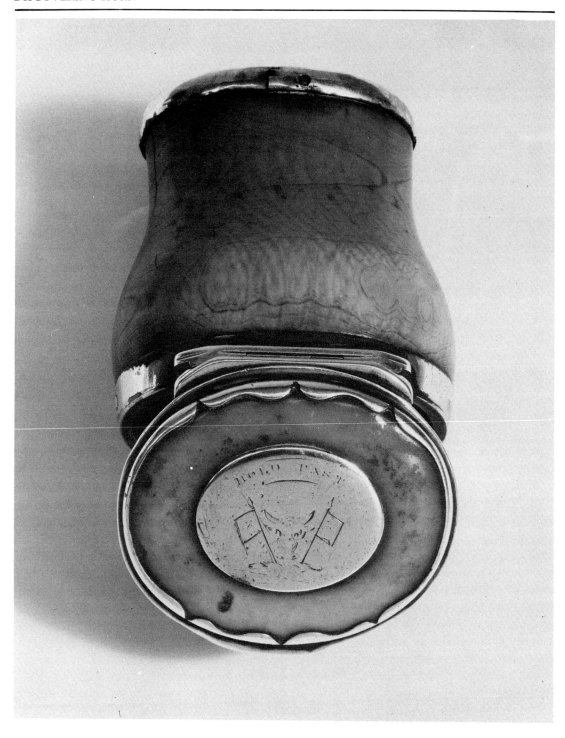

Eighteenth-century Jacobite style ivory mull with silver mounts bearing MacLeod Crest of the bull's head with the motto 'Hold Fast'. (Length: 6.5 cm.)

'It is recorded that while the St Margaret's Vestry Club were dining at Greenwich in 1805 the bitter-sweet news of the battle of Trafalgar and the death of Nelson came up the Thames, and at each subsequent anniversary dinner the toast "To the immortal memory of Nelson" was drunk in solemn silence.'

Thus the Overseers' Society inherited the right to use this solemn toast from 1906, and since that time it has continued to be proposed at the Society's annual dinner.

Then follows the time-honoured traditional ceremony of the annual transmission of the Westminster tobacco box with its cases. Since the official duties of Overseer ended in 1900 the safety of the box was in theory entrusted to two custodians. They serve for two successive years, first as junior custodian and then as senior custodian. The latter is responsible for the new ornament or engraving.

Perhaps the final comment on this historic box should be made in quotation from the opening of Harry How's article in the *Strand Magazine* of November 1894.

'Waal, sir,' remarked an enthusiastic gentleman from Nebraska to Mr J. E. Smith, the Vestry Clerk of Westminster. 'We can show you the biggest thing in waterfalls, rivers and mountains, and I guess we can beat you in fires and railway smash-ups; but we'll give in over tobacco boxes. This is the biggest, and I'll stake the entire States on that.'

The famous receptacle for the fragrant weed is not only the biggest in the world, but unquestionably an historical curiosity into the bargain.

RORY MOR HORN

Dunvegan castle, Isle of Skye, has been the stronghold of the chiefs of MacLeod for over seven hundred years and it remains a family home today. For their crest they have a bull's head with the motto 'Hold Fast', the origin of which is a delightful legendary tale which deserves to be told because of the existence of the Rory Mor horn – a magnificent specimen from a Kyloe bull, a fine breed of Hebridean cattle.

The tale tells of Malcolm, the third chief of the clan from about 1320–1370, who killed a bull in the wood of Glenelg because it had terrorized the local people. He is supposed to have used only his dirk for the battle with the bull. During the struggle one of the bull's horns was broken off. When Malcolm returned victorious to Dunvegan his trophy was made into a drinking horn, and a subsequent tradition grew up whereby each chief on his succession was 'obliged to drain to the bottom at one draught of whatever quality of liquor it was the fashion of his time to drink'. According to the Bannatyne ms, and papers preserved in the Dunvegan Charter Chest, the bull's head with the motto 'Hold Fast' was incorporated following Malcolm's feat, as onlookers cried 'Hold fast, MacLeod!'

Some sources suggest that Sir Rory 'Mor' MacLeod conceived the tradition of the chief drinking claret from the horn at his coming of age 'without setting down or falling down'. The horn holds a bottle and three quarters of claret!

It is possible to visit Dunvegan castle between Easter and mid October to see, amongst other treasures, the very beautiful horn given the name of the sixteenth chief and wrapped in the legendary history of the third chief Malcolm MacLeod of MacLeod.

Appendix III

British Horners of Today

ABBEY HORN

THE author is particularly grateful for much of the information given by John Barnes, the present owner of Abbey Horn, and also to Martin Scott, one of the directors. Like so many small craft firms Abbey Horn has relied on the passing from one generation to the next some of the vital traditional skills developed during many years of working horn. No detailed accounts have survived, although it is known that the original firm started in 1749 at Humpherson's of Bewdley, Worcestershire where it remained until 1912, coming then with Humpherson to Gloucester. At an unknown date Humpherson sold the Horn Works to a Mr Grove, who was a relation of the Grove Family, Halesowen. In turn, in about 1923, the Works were sold by Grove to Le Resche.

John Barnes bought the business in 1955 from Le Resche and Troughton and was fortunate enough to have Percy Le Resche stay on until his death a few years later. It was from Le Resche, a descendant from the Huguenots, that John Barnes heard so much of the Horn Works at Gloucester railway yard. It was Percy Le Resche who 'inspired by the signs of the railway sidings' property' had called the business in Llanthony Road 'Abbey' Horn Works after Llanthony Abbey, a favourite haunt of his tucked in the hills behind Hay-on-Wye, Herefordshire. For many years the firm's price lists bore an illustration of the entrance to Llanthony, although no hornworking was carried on there. The move to Kendal which has a castle but no abbey presented no problem to Le Resche. 'We'll keep the name,' he said. 'It won't be long before folks come to think Kendal has an abbey.'

The original Kendal combworks running on the water wheel power of the strong river Kent had operated for several generations. It was a thriving business with a healthy export market sending horn combs to the British colonies, but the advent of plastics took its toll of demand for genuine horn products and the Kendal combworks closed. Two of the Troughton family owning those combworks

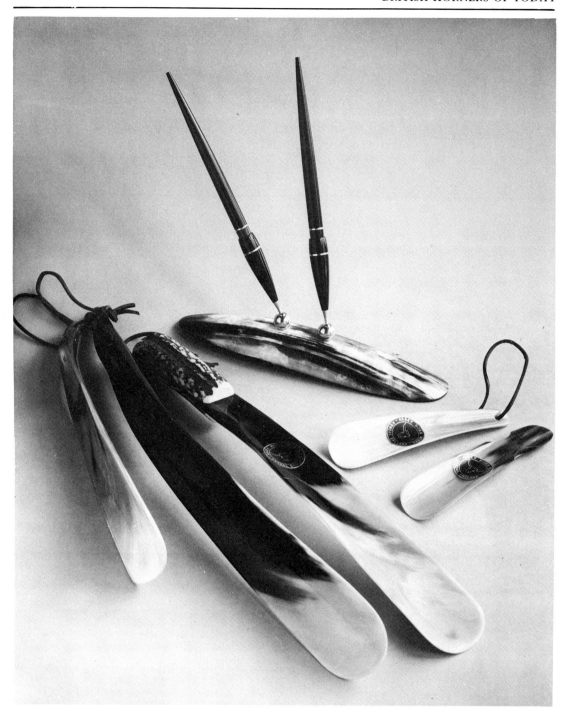

A selection of shoehorns and a penholder manufactured by Abbey Horn Works.

moved away, one to the comb factory at Milnthorpe, owned by W. P. Dobson, and the other to Abbey Horn in Gloucester, eventually forming a partnership with Le Resche. In 1940 the Abbey Horn Works of Gloucester moved to Kendal and the two brothers were reunited and worked together in the building still occupied today.

It was in talks with these three old horners that John Barnes learned much of the earlier days of Abbey Horn. Stories abound of itinerant Irishmen in Kendal working as 'breakers', opening horns heated by charcoal. The method was to heat the whole horn in a flame and by holding the horn with pliers against the leather apron a cut was made into the softened horn following the natural curve. Once the sharp knife had opened a gap pliers were forced into the opening, and by reheating and re-opening the horn a large flat plate was produced. This was placed between iron plates and screwed with others in a long vice until cool and set ready for cutting into comb blanks. The Irishmen would alternate between working at the horn factory and navvying on the Lancaster to Kendal canal. The horn combworks was a very useful place when navvying wages had been spent – mostly at the local inns. Some strength is needed to open and flatten horns and navvying certainly trained the arms well, but the working conditions contributed to a life span often short of forty years.

Le Resche often spoke of 'old Edwin' who had worked at Gloucester as a hornturner. Edwin specialized in turning horn beakers and could do so at great speed, but his enthusiasm did not extend to fitting bases to them and large piles of turned beakers with separate bases accumulated. Edwin could only be persuaded to bring the two together by cutting off the power to his lathe! He would then heat the lower part of the beaker and 'click-in' the base, working as slowly as possible and cursing the whole time.

Le Resche used to speak of the days just after the First World War when he would attend horn sales at London docks. Bales of African horns were neatly stacked in warehouses with many samples laid out on the floors. The price varied very little from year to year, unlike today's market prices.

John Barnes inherited a number of curious horn items which had formerly been produced by Abbey Horn. These included an opened scoop of jet black buffalo horn, a type which used to be supplied to a firm in Australia providing gold prospectors with 'pans'; a medicine beaker which was one of a pattern made for Florence Nightingale for use in the Crimean War, and an interesting curved horn plate with a couple of horn tabs which was used for fitting to the top of riding boots to enable breeches to tuck into the top.

The working conditions of the factory in the middle of the 1950s were very uncomfortable. There was little in the way of dust extraction or cleaning, with the result that the sawing and abrasive processes had shrouded everything in an ever-increasing layer of horn dust. The technical changes which have occurred since those days have made it possible to improve working conditions enormously. Modern full dust extraction machinery, new abrasives, new heating techniques and new polishes have all contributed to the horn work being undertaken in more comfortable surroundings with less hazards to the hornworkers.

Abbey Horn, who make a wide and appealing variety of objects sell their products not only in their own retail shops in the busy tourist centres of Kendal and Bowness but also throughout Britain. Besides this flourishing side of their business they have captured wide markets in America. They are some of the very few craftsmen who are able to produce translucent horn on the world market today. This product is used by antique dealers and restorers both in this country and abroad for clock casings, lanthorn leaves and furniture repairs.

CORNUCOPIA

This two-partner organization certainly lives up to its name. Adele Schaverien and Margaret Bunford met when starting one of the early Decorative and Fine Art Societies and realized they both had a desire to take a more direct and practical interest in connection with the fine arts.

Following the Worshipful Company of Horners' dinner in the Autumn of 1976 Adele's husband, Bernard, who is a member, suggested she should try her hand at hornworking. Further encouraged by the late Gordon Pinker, Past Master of the Horners' Company, she and her friend started Cornucopia in May 1977 in Northwood, Middlesex.

Adele and Margaret were granted the Freedom of the Company as working lady horners in 1977 and it is believed they are the first, certainly recorded, since the eighteenth century.

Fine quality oxhorn drinking horns silver gilt mounted with the eagle's clawfoot.

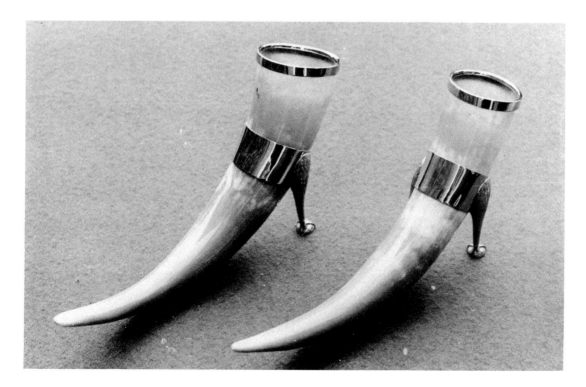

The designs for the enchanting articles which they make develop from mutual discussion and agreement and at a later stage with their silversmith, Melvyn Kemp. The designs include silver gilt or silver-mounted drinking horns – with either the Romanesque foot (not unlike the Pusey horn foot) or the eagle's claw – and trinket or pill boxes which may be either silver-mounted alone or have, in addition, a gemstone mount. The designs for the feet of the drinking horns were originally made by Bernard Schaverien in child's modelling clay, but the silversmith asked for them to be made in brass – a very exacting request, but one fulfilled by Bernard with immense effort and care which combined with the work of the silversmith has helped to produce articles to a very high standard.

It was in the Spring of 1977 that their own sponsors' mark was granted by the Goldsmiths' Company. This was rather an exciting year, for their articles could bear their sponsors' mark AS & MB and the Jubilee mark. It is possible to request for special shields and engraving work to be undertaken on the mounts, and the customer is also encouraged to discuss the choice of horn for its toning and colour blends, which vary considerably from one oxhorn to another.

The basic hornwork is undertaken by Cornucopia using the traditional methods of heating, cutting, pressing and polishing, as well as certain preparations which produce a good, rich lustre, without the unattractive high gloss often found on modern articles, many of which come from abroad.

Cornucopia is a registered partnership now based at Westcote, Dunsfold, Surrey, working entirely on a commission basis and it is perhaps sufficient to say that the firm has exhibited at the Goldsmiths' Company Loot Exhibition in London and also that some of their items were accepted for the Goldsmiths' Loot Minneapolis Exhibition in July 1978. Clearly their work will appeal to the connoisseur and the collector in the knowledge that the articles from this source will surely be among the antiques of the future.

THE GROVE FAMILY, HALESOWEN

The names Grove and Halesowen have been synonymous for a great number of years, but it was not until 1857 that James Grove started his own business as a manufacturer of horn buttons. Since that date the firm has become a large and prosperous business incorporating the Stour Fertilizer Company Ltd, who deal with all the horn waste and hooves by grinding them to powder and sending the bagged products to the fertilizer industry. The powder is also sold for protein in animal feeds, for part of the construction of wall boards in the building industry and as part of the compound material for fire-fighting foam, particularly for airfields.

In 1939, Frank Horn of Cologne who, with others until that time had run an import merchants business, approached the Grove firm, who had bought and sold from them, to ask if they would be willing to finance a business in Halesowen because of difficult trading conditions in Germany. The Grove firm guaranteed £3,000 and in August of the same year the Halesowen Horn Company was incorporated using the name of the original owner from Cologne. From the beginning the Grove family sat on the board, and Frank Horn senior, as a managing director, continued his raw horn business.

The firm survived the war and in the early 1950s Frank Horn senior once again approached the Grove family to ask if his son, Frank Horn junior, who was then in Australia, could join the board and take over as managing director. This was agreed and during the next three decades this subsidiary company of the Grove family manufactured hornware; some articles are made totally on the premises, while others are bought in from both Scotland and abroad. The present Frank Horn, the acknowledged expert in horn definition, partially retired in 1979 and now deals only with raw horn material, buying and selling from overseas to any wholesalers on an international basis.

There is now a sales manager who organizes the goods for the retail trade, has agents, and supplies mail order firms. The articles are very diverse and many of them are particularly attractive, a speciality being full-rigged sailing ships of varying sizes.

The tip end of buffalo horn being subjected to an electrical saw for cutting button shapes, leaving only the tip which is used as a toggle.

Alphabetical List of Horn Artefacts

Bobbins
Books – horn
Boxes –
   card
   patch
   sewing
   snuff
   tinder
   tobacco
   trinket
Beakers
Busks
Buttons
Butts
Candlesticks
Cardcases
Ceremonial horns
Chairs
Chalices
Cigar cutters
Cigarette holders
Combs
Composite bows
Corkscrew handles
Crossbows
Cruets
Dagger handles
Dishes
Drenching horns
Drinking horns
Egg cups
Fans
Farrier's searching knives

Fish lures
Flasks
Fleams
Flower vases
Golf club putters
Gramophone needles
Grease horns
Handles
Horn books
Inkhorns
Jewellery
Jewellery caskets
Knife handles
Labels – wine and spirit
Ladles – punch and toddy
Lanthorn leaves
Laundry tallies
Libation cups
Measuring beakers
Musical instruments
Napkin rings
Needle case covers
Needle horns
Notebooks (*aides-mémoire*
   with covers of horn)
Nutmeg graters
Ornaments
Paper knives
Pen holders
Pipes and pipe stems
Penknife scales
Picture frames
Plaques

Pounce pots
Powder flasks
Powder horns
Priming horns
Quaichs
Quill cutters
Quill holders
Reading glass frames
Rings
Salad servers
Sanding horns
Scales
Scoops
Seeding horns
Shoe horns
Shofarot
Slip trail horns
Snuff mulls
Sounding horns
Spoons and ladles
Stirrup cups
Sword hilts and scabbards
Tampers
Tatting shuttles
Tea caddies
Tools
Tree scribes
Vestas
Vinaigrettes
Walking stick handles
Watch cases
Whistles
Writing compendiums

Appendix V

Glossary

ANTLERS, which are made of solid bone without any epidermal covering and are processes of the frontal bone, come from the cervidae group of animals. They are shed and renewed annually.

BAKELITE was patented in 1909 by the inventor Leo H. Baekeland, a Belgian living in the USA. Bakelite is a hard infusible plastic made into a carbon compound from formaldehyde and Phenol B. Imitations were made of ivory, horn, bone and tortoiseshell which was mass-produced by pressure and heat on yellow plates between plates coloured with brown and compacted. *See* Mockshell and Celluloid.

BLACK HORN may be achieved by applying silver nitrate which, if exposed to the sun, turns the article to jet black. It may also be the natural state of the horn.

BONE is a fairly distinctive natural material although it is sometimes mistaken for ivory by the inexperienced eye. The fairly reliable visual support is given by the tell-tale short interrupted dark line marks. Bone also has a drier, harder feel than ivory.

BOVIDAE group includes cattle, goats, sheep, African antelopes. Horns are present on males and often on females.

BRISÉ fan is so described because it has no leaf. The fan consists of sticks of some stiff material, e.g. horn or tortoiseshell joined by means of an interwoven looped ribbon.

CASEIN, which is part of the structure of bone, is used in moulding to imitate many genuine materials including horn, ivory and tortoiseshell. It is very rubbery in its form and lacks the lustre of the natural material.

CELLULOID was invented by John Wesley Hyatt of the USA in 1869. It is a highly flammable material made from a prepared mixture of cellulose nitrate and camphor. It is very tough and is resistant to water, oils, and dilute acids. During the last third of the nineteenth century it was used extensively for the world-wide production of highly commercial goods, including combs, boxes, spoons, and toys. It was replaced in some commercial areas by less flammable but similar materials. Nevertheless it is still used in the manufacture of certain goods today. *See* Bakelite and Parkesine.

CELLULOSE is extracted from the fibrous parts of trees and shrubs and it is from a process of nitration that cellulose is developed into the celluloid solid material for manufacture, known as cellulose nitrate. *See* Parkesine and Bakelite and Celluloid.

CELLULOSE NITRATE, *see* Cellulose.

CERVIDAE include the deer which carry solid bone antlers which are shed and renewed each year.

CHAMPLEVÉ enamel in which colours are filled into hollows made in the surface (Fr. raised field).

CORE, *see* Pith.

DENTINE is a hard tissue which is the chief constituent of teeth and tusks. It is not unlike bone but is usually more dense and is made up of minute tubes and cells. *See* Ivory.

DRAGON'S BLOOD is an odourless resin found on the fruits of certain trees native to Sumatra and Borneo. It is collected and formed into solid cakes for export purposes. Before being used these cakes are reduced to powder which is a brilliant red in colour.

GESSO – plaster of paris – prepared for use in sculpture and in painting.

GREENHORN must be given three definitions. In one sense it is used by horners to describe poor quality horn in its raw state; in the second it is the term used by horners for the transparent horn which results through boiling and removing of the natural colour so that dyeing or staining could then be undertaken; in the third it is the term used for specifically green dyed horn. *See* Translucent horn.

HAFTING is the insertion of a metal tip into the central cavity of a handle.

HARTSHORN substance obtained from deerhorn, formerly chief source of ammonia – and used for smelling salts.

HORN. The word is derived from Old English, Old Saxon, Old High German, Old Nordic. The Gothic *haurn*; from German *hornaz*; Latin *cornu*; Hebrew *qiren-keren*. Horn is the outer membrane of bone core, a process which grows on the upper part of the skull of bovidae and certain hoofed mammals. *See* Keratin.

HORN PLATE is made from horn, first split, then heated and flattened under pressure. As horn is stratified, a short round–nosed knife called a lift is inserted in edge of plate and *scales* or *leaves* may be raised. These transparent leaves were used for many purposes especially for the lanthorn (lantern).

HORNFLY is a serious pest which breeds in dung within two or three days and then clusters at the base of horns, causing intense irritation and inflammation to the animals.

IVORY consists mainly of calcium and phosphate and in transverse section shows lines of different colours. It is a variety of dentine, the most prized coming from the tusk of the elephant because of its durability. Vegetable ivory, also used commercially, comes from the corrozo nuts' seeds which grow on a palm-like tree of the Andes.

In 1856 Sir Richard Owen described ivory in one of his lectures as 'the hard white elastic and fine-grained substance (being dentine of exceptional hardness) composing the main part of the tusks of the elephant'. It is the close and compact pores which contain a gelatine type substance. This helps to produce the fine polish on the finished article. *See* Casein and Bone.

KERATIN. Keratin is a fibrous protein containing calcium and sulphur which is insoluble in most agents and will only smoulder when subjected to intense heat. As it is a nitrogenous substance forming the basis of horns the fertilizer industries use it in their mixtures. There is therefore no wastage from the horn work as all shavings and poor quality horns or hooves are ground and sterilized before sale to manufacturers.

LACQUER, *see* Veneer.

LOGWOOD CHIP (buckthorn family). Chippings from the American logwood tree which yields a dye may be boiled in water to which a walnut-sized piece of ammonia is added and the whole is allowed to boil gently, resulting in a port wine dye colouring. Certain mineral salts may be added which produce a variety of shades of amber, red, blue or green.

MAUCHLINE-TYPE HINGE. The term 'mauchline hinge' was adopted because many boxes with this type of hinge were made in the Scottish town of that name.

MOCKSHELL is simulated tortoiseshell made from translucent oxhorn. Distributed in enormous quantities both at home and overseas in the first quarter of the nineteenth century by the firm of Dobson of Bradford, later of Milnthorpe, Kendal. Listed as mockshell in the inventories, it included deliveries to Sheffield, Liverpool, Birmingham, London, Yarmouth, Philadelphia, Nova Scotia, Montevideo and Leipzig. Mockshell lacks the three-dimensional qualities seen in the real tortoiseshell and this phenomenon is highlighted with an ultra-violet ray on to the shell in a darkened room. The high quality staining is sometimes very difficult to tell from the real thing but magnification to ×10 usually indicates a fault if examined over a wide area. *See* Tortoiseshell and Casein.

OXHORN – the generic term used nowadays to cover the horns from the ruminant group of animals of the bison, bull, cow and ox.

PARKESINE. Alexander Parkes, a British inventor, won a bronze medal in 1862 for the invention of parkesine which is 'a substance as hard as horn, but as flexible as leather, capable of being cast or stamped, painted, dyed, carved'. It may be distinguished from horn by its somewhat 'dead' appearance with a feel and sound of plastic. *See* Celluloid and Bakelite.

PATCH BOX is a receptacle in the side of a rifle butt designed to hold grease patches or small pieces of equipment.

PENCIL TANG is a thin projection of metal which is extended through the handle, the tip end of which is often covered with a metal cap.

PIQUÉ work is applied metalwork and mother of pearl on an alternative material.

PITH is the porous outgrowth of bone contained within the horn. When dried naturally in hot climates the pith may be used industrially for the manufacture of glues and gelatines. During the 1939–1945 war an extract from this was used by the soap industry.

ROTTENSTONE is decomposed siliceous limestone, used as polishing powder. *See* Talc.

SCALE is a slab or slice of a piece of horn fixed on either side of a metal tang in the central position.

SIMULATED TORTOISESHELL, *see* Mockshell.

SOAPSTONE is an impure form of talc sometimes used for making ornaments and boxes.

TALC magnesium silicate, one of the softest minerals, when ground to a powder is used as a lubricator. Pure talc has a greasy, soapy feel. It is found in transparent plates and sometimes used as a glazing material.

TALLOW is a substance obtained by melting the harder and less fusible kinds of fat from animals.

TANG is a point or projection which extends into a handle. The tang may be a pencil thickness or a wedge slice.

TINE – a point on an antler or the prong of a fork.

TORTOISESHELL, which contains keratin, consists of the epidermic plates covering the bony skeleton of the marine hawksbill turtle, *Eretmochelys imbricata*. The finest tortoiseshell comes from the Eastern Archipelago (Molucca Sea). The highly prized plates of the back of the animal number thirteen and consist of horny matter, but when examined under the microscope are seen to be made up of small, spherical scales in reticular form containing a reddish brown pigment. Tortoiseshell is worked in a manner similar to horn, but at a lower temperature as high heat tends to darken and camouflage the highly sought after richly mottled tones. Unlike horn, tortoiseshell may be thickened or increased in size by carefully cleaning and rasping the surfaces to be joined, heating the plates and then pressing them tightly together. The heat liquifies the surface film and thus when united the plates make a perfect join.

A close imitation of tortoiseshell may be made by staining translucent oxhorn and it is interesting to note that in the inventories of Dobson, horner, there are numerous entries listing Mockshell plates, card-cases, combs, combcases and segar (cigar) cases for Baltic trade and for Russia. *See* Mockshell.

TRANSLUCENT OR TRANSPARENT HORN. A term sometimes used to define greenhorn, i.e. when natural colour has been removed. When heated horn is pressed at great pressure in a heated vice, many of which are hydraulic today, the laminations are compacted, which gives the horn extra strength. It also develops a greenish translucent hue as a result of the heat and removal of the sulphur. Longhorn is sometimes found to be translucent when the outer skin is removed providing the horn is of a faultless texture. Finer translucency is achieved by scraping the horn as thin as desirable. *See* Greenhorn.

VELLUM is a fine parchment originally made from the skin of a calf.

VENEER. A veneer of either horn or tortoiseshell may be achieved by covering its under surface with a coating of lampblack and fish glue. A piece of paper is then placed on this cement, to which it adheres. The papered surface of the horn substance is then glued on to the wood in the same manner as other veneers. The object of the cement and paper is to develop the transparent effect of the horny material, by hiding the grain of the wood beneath.

VERDIGRIS, a green dye made from copper plates with the addition of acid juices treated in a specific manner.

WEEVIL. A type of beetle which attacks dead horn left in damp conditions. It is suggested by Bob Child, Senior Conservation Officer at St Fagan's Folk Museum, that this beetle is the furry beetle which may be treated with thiamole crystals enclosed with the endangered article in a bag. It has also been established that horn comes to no harm when treated with liquid Rentokil used in the same way as on furniture.

WHITE HORN is horn with its natural colour, a much sought after natural condition.

YELLOWED HORN is achieved by placing the green horn in boiling water to which some nitric acid has been added. This creates a deep and permanent yellow stain.

184

Appendix VI

Bibliography

ALDERSON, L. *The Observer's Book of Farm Animals*, Frederick Warne & Co Ltd, 1976.

ARMSTRONG, N. *A Collectors' History of Fans*, Cassell and Collier, 1974.

BAGSHAWE, T. W. 'Engraved Horn Mugs', *Apollo* XXVII, 1938, pp. 254–257.

BICKERTON, L. M. 'The Horner's Craft', *Country Life*, 1973, pp. 1627–1628.

BICKERTON, L. M. *The Horner's Craft Catalogue*, Worthing Museum Publication, 1973.

BONSER, K. J. *The Drovers*, Macmillan, 1970.

BOOK OF ENGLISH TRADES AND LIBRARY OF THE USEFUL ARTS, London, 1824.

BRAGGE, W. *Bibliotheca Nicotiana*, Birmingham, 1880.

BRAGGE, W. *Illustrated Catalogue (No. 409) of Bibliotheca Nicotiana*, Birmingham, 1880.

BRIDGE, J. C. 'Horns' in *Journal of the Architectural, Archaeological, and Historical Society of Chester*, 1904, pp. 86–166.

BRINK, F. H. VAN DEN *A Field Guild to the Mammals of Britain and Europe*, Collins, 1967.

BURNETT, J. *A History of the Cost of Living*, Penguin, 1969.

CAMPBELL *The London Tradesman*, 1747, facsimile edition by David and Charles, 1969.

CARTER, T. D. *Hoofed Mammals of the World*, Lutterworth Press, 1974.

CELSUS. A. A. C. *De Medicina*. First printed in 1478.

CHAPLIN, R. E. *Deer*, (Mammal Series), Blandford, 1977.

CHURCH, A. H. *Some Minor Arts*, Seeley & Co, 1894 (*see* READ).

CITY OF WESTMINSTER *Some Account of the Westminster Tobacco Box; The Westminster Cigar Box; The Westminster Snuff Box and other Muniment Insignia*, Wightman Ltd, 1900.

C.K. *Arts Masterpiece*, 1697.

COLYER, R. J. *The Welsh Cattle Drovers*, University of Wales Press, 1976.

COLLYER, J. *The Parents and Guardians Directory of a Profession or Trade*, 1761.

COMPTON, C. H. *The Worshipful Company of Horners of London*, Collingridge, 1882.

CORBEILLER, C. DE *European and American Snuff Boxes* (1730–1830), Batsford, 1966.

COUPER, T. G. 'Horn Fashioned by Craftsmen', *Scotland's Magazine*, 1965, Vol. 61, pp. 46–48.

CROWELL, I. H. *Horn Craft*, Macmillan, 1945.

CURTIS, M. *The Book of Snuff and Snuff Boxes*, Peter Owen, 1956.

DANIEL, M. 'Planting the Penny Hedge', *Country Life Magazine*, 1975, Vol. CLVII, p. 1128.

DICTIONARIUM POLYGRAPHICUM (1735).

DIDEROT *Encyclopédie*, 1763.

DREIER, F. A. *Berichte ausden Staatlichen Museen des Preussischen Kulturbesitzes*, 1968 (Nette Folge XVIII, Heft 2).

DREW, J. H. *The Horn Comb Industry of Kenilworth*, Birmingham Archaeological Society, 1965.

DUNCAN, R. 'Horn Carver of Braemar', *Scotland's Magazine*, 1957, May, pp. 29–31.

FEDDEN, R. 'John Obrisset', *The Connoisseur*, 1972, Vol. 180, pp. 13–17.

FISHER, F. J. *A Short History of the Worshipful Company of Horners*, 1936.

FLAUENSGAARD, E. B. AND J. *Working in Plastic, Bone, Amber and Horn*, Reinhold Book Corporation, 1968.

GRANCSAY, S. V. *American Engraved Powder Horns*, Riling, 1945.

GRANT, I. F. *The History of a Clan 1200–1256*, Faber, 1959.

GREEN, B. DE VERE *A Collector's Guide to Fans over the Ages*, Muller, 1975.

GRIFFIN, A. H. *The Story of Abbey Horn*, Titus Wilson, Kendal.

GRUNDY, A. H. 'Rhinoceros Horn Cups', *Apollo*, 1963, Vol. 129.

GUTHMAN, W. H. 'Powder Horns of the French and Indian War', *Antiques*, The Magazine Publishers' Association, USA, 1978.

HACKENBROCH, Y. 'A Limoge Enamel Hunting Horn', *The Connoisseur*, 1954, Vol. CXXXIII.

HANSMANN, L. AND L. K. RETTENBECK *Amulett und Talismann*, Verlag Georg D. W. Callwey, Munich, pp. 126–128, 1977.

HARLEY, R. D. *Artists' Pigments 1600–1835*, Butterworth, 1970.

HARRISON, W. *Millenary Book of Ripon*, Harrison Publishers, Ripon, 1892.

HARTLEY, D. *Made in England*, Methuen, 1937.

HARTLEY, D. *The Horn Workers*, Methuen, 1933.

HOLLAND, J. *Brief Notes of Animal Substances used in the Sheffield Manufactures*, Ridge & Jackson, 1840.

HOMBERG, F. *Process for the Treatment of Horn or the Like*, United States Patent Office 1,636,818, 1927.

HOW, H. 'The Biggest Tobacco-Box in the World', *The Strand Magazine*, 1894.

HUGHES, G. B. *Living Crafts*, Lutterworth Press, 1953.

INTERPRETERS *Dictionary of the Bible*, K–Q, Abingdon Press, 1962.

JAMES, M. R. 'The Earliest Inventory of Corpus Christi College', pp. 88–114. *Proceedings Cambridge Antiquarian Society*. NS10, 1912.

JENYNS, R. S. *Chinese Art*, The Minor Arts II, pp. 189–218, Oldbourne Press, 1965.

JERVIS, SIMON 'Furniture in Horn and Antler', *Connoisseur*, November, 1977, pp. 190–201.

JONES, E. A. *The Old Plate of the Cambridge Colleges*, p. 40, Cambridge, 1910.

JONES, S. 'The Waigal Horn Chair', *Man* Magazine, pp. 253–7, 1970.

KREUNITZ, J. G. *Oeconomische Encyclopaedie oder allgemeines system der land -haus -und staatswirtschaft*, Vol. 25, 1789.

LEJARD, ANDRÉ *The Bayeux Tapestry*, Parrish, London, 1947.

MACLEOD OF MACLEOD, R. G. *The MacLeods of Dunvegan*, Printed privately by the Clan MacLeod Society, 1927.

MANN, J. G. 'The Horn of St Hubert', *The Burlington Magazine*, Vol. XCII, 1950, Nos. 562–573.

MEYERS, *Konversationslexikon*, Bibliographisches Institut, Leipzig und Wein, 1898.

MILLER, H. (Ed.) *Permanent and Loan Collections of the Jewish Museum*, London, 1974.

OMAN, C. C. 'English Medieval Drinking Horns', *The Connoisseur*, 1944, Vol. CXIII.

OMAN, C. *Cambridge & Cornelimunster*, pp. 305–6, Aachener Kunstblätter 43, 1972.

OSWALD, A. 'A Relic of Feudal Times – the Tutbury Horn', *Country Life*, Vol. 129, 1961, p. 582.

PARKER, A. 'The Bewdley Horn Industry in Worcestershire', *Naturalists' Club Transactions*, 1947, Vol. 10, pp. 107–108.

PEARCE, M. 'Collecting Sheffield Cut-Throat Razors', *Antique Collector*, 1977, Vol. 12, No. 3.

PERCIVAL, M. *The Fan Book*, Fisher Unwin, 1920.

PERRY, R. *The Watcher and the Red Deer*, Country Book Club, Newton Abbot, 1952.

PHILLIPS, P. A. S. *John Obrisset*, Batsford, 1931.

POLLER, T. H. A. *The Use of Horn in the Decoration of Louis XV Pendules*, Private monograph, 1979.

PROCEEDINGS OF THE SOCIETY OF ANTIQUARIES OF SCOTLAND: 1866–1868, Vol. 7, pp. 116+561–2; 1876–1878, Vol. 12, pp. 458–9; 1882–1883, Vol. 17, pp. 455–6.

RAWSON, J. *Animals in Art*, British Museum Publications Ltd, 1977.

READ, C. H., FSA *English Work in Impressed Horn*, 1894 (*see* CHURCH).

RILING, R. *The Powder Flask Book*, Bonanza Books, USA, 1953.

RITCHIE, C. I. A. *Scrimshaw*, Oak Tree Press, 1972.

RITCHIE, C. I. A. *Bone and Horn Carving*, Thomas Yoseloff Ltd, 1975.

ROES, A. 'Horn Cheek Pieces', *Antiquaries Journal*, Vol. 40, 1960, pp. 68–72.

ROSEDALE, H. G. *Some Notes of the Old Book of the Worshipful Company of Horners*, London, the Company, 1911.

ROSEDALE, H. G. *A Short History of the Worshipful Company of Horners*, London, Blade, 1912.

ROUBO, M. *L'Art du Menuisier*, Paris, 1774, p. 987.

ROUGIER, J. W. *Recollections of Hornworking in York*, Huguenot Society of London, 1963, pp. 454–6.

SMITH, G. F. H. *Gemstones*, Methuen, 1912.

SMITH, J. E. *The Westminster Box*, Westminster, 1887.

SMITH, J. E. *St John the Evangelist*, Parochial Memorials, Westminster, 1892.

SPEARMAN, R. I. C. *The Integument*, CUP, 1973.

STALKER, J. *Art of Japanning*, 1688, facsimile edition, Tiranti, London, 1960.

STEEDS, W. *A History of Machine Tools*, OUP, 1969.

STEPHENSON, SIMON Representations of the Embossed, Chased and Engraved Subjects and Inscriptions which decorate the Tobacco Box and Cases belonging to the Past Overseers Society of the Parishes of St Margaret and St John the Evangelist in the City of Westminster. I. Clark, Westminster, 1824.

STONE, P. 'Some Famous Drinking Horns in Britain', *Apollo*, 1961, Volume 74.

STONE, P. 'When Children Read From Horn Books', *Country Life*, 1961, Vol. CXXX, pp. 941–43.

TARDY *La Pendule Français*, Paris, 1949.

TAYLOR, W. *The Sheffield Horn Industry*, J. W. Northend Ltd, 1927.

THIEL, P. J. J. VAN *John Osborn*, Miscellanes J. Q. van Regteren Altens, Amsterdam, 1969, pp. 104–110 and 308–310.

TOMLINSON, C. *Cyclopaedia of Useful Arts* (part V, 1853), pp. 20–21, 'Horn'.

TUER, A. W. *History of the Horn Book*, Vol. I and II. Leadenhall Press, 1896.

TULIP, N. *The Art of Stick Dressing*, F. Graham, Newcastle, 1978.

UNWIN, G. *The Gilds of London*, Frank Cass & Co, 1908.

WALCOTT, M. E. C. *Westminster*, Masters, 1849.

WENHAM, L. P. *Hornpot Lane and the Horners of York*, Yorkshire Philosophical Society, 1964.

WHITLOCK, R. *Bulls Through the Ages*, Lutterworth Press, 1977.

WORSLEY, A. V. *Hornchurch Parish Church – A History*, printed by Benham, Colchester, 1964.

WUNSCH, T. V. S. *Ivory, Bone and Horn Cutting*, Macmillan, 1945.

ZIM, H. S. AND SHAFFER, P. R. *Rocks and Minerals*, Paul Hamlyn, 1965.

Acknowledgements

The author would like to thank the following institutions and individuals for their valued help in providing information and material for this book.

Museums and Art Galleries: James Dun's House, Aberdeen; Bewdley Museum, Worcestershire; Birmingham City Museum and Art Gallery; Moyse's Hall Museum, Bury St Edmunds, Suffolk; Bishop Hooper's Lodging, Gloucester; Hereford City Museum and Art Gallery; British Museum, London; British Museum (Natural History), London; Jewish Museum, London; The Museum of London; Tower of London; University College Museum of Zoology and Comparative Anatomy, London; Victoria and Albert Museum, London; Wallace Collection, London; Wellcome Historical Medical Museum, London; Pitt Rivers Museum, Oxford; Perth Museum and Art Gallery; Plymouth City Museum and Buckland Abbey; Portsmouth Royal Naval Museum; Sheffield City Museum; National Museum of Antiquities of Scotland, Edinburgh; National Museum of Wales, Cardiff; Welsh Folk Museum, St Fagans; Worthing Museum, Sussex; Castle Museum, York; Hartlebury Castle, Hereford and Worcester County Museum.

Libraries: Central Library, Aberdeen; Haslemere Library, Surrey; British Library, London; Guildhall Library, London; Westminster Abbey Library, London; Westminster City Library, London; Bodleian Library, Oxford; Worthing Reference Library, Sussex.

Other Organizations: The Abbey Hornworks, Kendal, Cumbria; Benmuir, Photograph Services Ltd, Camberley (colour photography and monochrome photography); Cornucopia, Dunsfold, Surrey; Corpus Christi College, Cambridge; The Grove Family, Halesowen, Birmingham; Lloyds Bank, Economic Adviser's Department; The Past Overseers' Society; The Worshipful Company of Horners; The Worshipful Company of Clockmakers.

Individuals: Len Bickerton, retired curator of Worthing Museum; Hillary Corney, silversmith, Petersfield; David Eggins, Lord Mayor Treloar College, for translating German manuscripts; Ralph Ewart and Patrick Hamilton for help with photographic printing; Mr Harding, Sergeant, Ripon Town Hall; Adrian Hardwick, for diagrams and sketches; Christopher Hardwick, for monochrome photography; Lord Mayor's Secretary, City Hall, Westminster; The Chief of the Clan MacLeod of MacLeod; Lionel Monro; Robert Noble, Charterhouse, for translating French manuscripts; Martyn O'Kelly, Farnham (colour photography and monochrome photography); The late Gordon Pinker, past Master, Horners' Company and Mrs Joan Pinker; Stephen Price, for access to notes on Bewdley horn industry; John Richmond, Mayor of Ripon, 1975; William Steele, stick dresser, Dorset; George Stooke-Vaughan, Antique dealer, Petersfield; Ann Wragge Morley, for line drawings; Margaret Wragge Morley, for typing manuscript; Peter Wragge Morley, St Edmund's School, Hindhead, for translating Latin manuscripts; Arthur Clemson.

Illustration Acknowledgements

The author would also like to thank the following for permission to reproduce the illustrations and artefacts appearing in this book.

Bodleian Library, Oxford: 84 left (A.f.11) right (A.f.80); *British Museum, London:* 11 left; *W. Brown private collection:* 135; *Christie's, South Kensington:* 153, 154; *Clemson private collection:* 66 above, 80; *Clinkers Antiques Ltd:* 116 right, 120 below; *Jim Furner:* Title page; *Halesowen Horn Works:* 21 above and below, 179; *Hereford City Museum and Art Gallery:* 68 below; *Horn Antiques:* 36 above, 38, 40, 42, 44, 57, 58 left, 60 left, 61, 66 below, 68 above, 70 above, 71 left, 82, 83, 89, 90 right, 90 below right, 91, 92 above and below, 93, 100, 103, 104 above right, 107, 109, 110, 112, 113, 116 left and below, 117, 118 below left, 119, 120 left, 121 above, 122, 123, 124, 125, 126, 128, 130, 133, 134, 137, 138, 141 above, 143, 144, 145 above, 150, 151, 172; *Jewish Museum:* 44 below, 45; *The Museum of London:* 85 left, 96; *The Late Charles Morse private collection:* 118 above; *Moyse's Hall Museum:* 29; *National Museum of Antiquities of Scotland, Edinburgh:* 11 right, 33 left, centre and right, 36, 39, 58 right, 59, 92 right, 139 left; *Perth Museum and Art Gallery:* 24 left and right, 90 above left, centre and right; *Pinker private collection:* 71 below, 79; *Pitt Rivers Museum, Oxford:* 75; *H. F. Russell private collection:* 141 below; *Schaverien Collection:* 81; *Antony Sidgwick:* 28; *Derek Smith, Kendal:* 14 left and right, 37, 127, 175; *Spink and Son Ltd:* 34, 114, 115; *Victoria and Albert Museum:* half title page, 31, 35, 78; *Wallace Collection, London:* 48; *Welsh Folk Museum, St Fagan's:* 108, 139 above; *The Worshipful Company of Clockmakers:* 73, 74; *The Worshipful Company of Horners:* 60 right, 62, 63, 64, 70 below, 76, 94, 97, 98, 99, 101, 102, 104 below left and right, 110 above, 131 left above, 140 above, 142; *Castle Museum, York:* 69, 72, 85 right, 121 left.

Index

Figures in **bold** type refer to illustrations